Table of Contents

Introduction:
1. Understanding the Power of Conversational AI
   1.1 Evolution of Chatbots and Conversational AI
   1.2 Introduction to GPT (Generative Pre-trained Transformer)
   1.3 Overview of GPT-4 Chat – Newest Conversational AI Model
   1.4 The Potential and Real-World Applications of GPT-4 Chat

Part I: Getting Started with GPT-4 Chat
2. Setting up your Environment
   2.1 Hardware and Software Requirements
   2.2 Installation and Configuration Steps
   2.3 Familiarizing with the GPT-4 Chat Interface

3. Navigating the GPT-4 Chat Interface
   3.1 Exploring the User Interface Components
   3.2 Understanding the Input and Output Format
   3.3 Accessing Advanced Settings and Options
   3.4 Interacting with the Model via API

Part II: Leveraging GPT-4 Chat Capabilities
4. Preparing High-Quality Input

4.1 Crafting Contextual Prompts for Effective Conversations

4.2 Utilizing System and User Messages

4.3 Incorporating Context from Past Conversations

4.4 Handling Sensitive Topics and Bias in Inputs

5. Navigating GPT-4 Chat Responses

5.1 Analyzing GPT-4 Chat Output Structure

5.2 Evaluating Response Coherence and Consistency

5.3 Optimizing for Desired Response Length

5.4 Transforming Model Outputs into User-Friendly Text

6. Expanding GPT-4 Chat Knowledge and Capabilities

6.1 Fine-Tuning GPT-4 Chat for Custom Domains

6.2 Incorporating External Knowledge Databases

6.3 Enhancing GPT-4 Chat's Specific Skills

6.4 Managing and Training Custom Datasets

Part III: Best Practices for Effective Conversational AI

7. Designing Engaging and User-Centric Conversations

7.1 Developing Conversation Flows and Structures

7.2 Handling Multiple Turns and Context Transitions

7.3 Planning Dynamic and Interactive User Interactions

7.4 Incorporating Personality and Tone in Conversations

8. Addressing Ethical Considerations and Bias

8.1 Ensuring Fairness and Bias Mitigation

8.2 Handling Sensitive and Offensive Content

8.3 Implementing User Consent and Privacy Measures

8.4 Ethical Implications of Open-Ended Conversations

9. Evaluating and Iterating Conversational AI Models

9.1 Designing Evaluation Metrics for Model Performance

9.2 Collecting User Feedback for Model Improvement

9.3 Iterating and Incrementally Enhancing Conversational AI

10. Real-world applications and Use Cases

10.1 Customer Support and Chatbots

10.2 Virtual Assistants and Personalized Interactions

10.3 Gaming and Interactive Storytelling

10.4 Educational and Language Learning Tools

10.5 Future Possibilities and Industry Adoption

Conclusion and Future Outlook:

11. Recap of Key Concepts and Takeaways

12. The Future of Conversational AI and GPT

13. Challenges and Opportunities for AI Researchers and Developers

Acknowledgment

Introduction

1. Understanding the Power of Conversational AI

In this era of rapidly evolving technology, Conversational AI has emerged as a powerful tool that is transforming the way we interact with machines. From virtual assistants like Siri and Alexa to customer service chatbots, Conversational AI enables machines to understand and respond to human language, making it possible for us to have natural and meaningful conversations with machines.

The aim of this book is to provide beginners with a comprehensive understanding of Conversational AI, its underlying technologies, and its vast potential in various domains. We will dive deep into the concepts, challenges, and applications of Conversational AI, equipping readers with the knowledge needed to appreciate and harness its power.

The chapter will start by discussing the history of Conversational AI, tracing its roots back to the early days of computer science and the development of Natural Language Processing.

We will explore how, over time, Conversational AI has evolved from simple rule-based systems to the sophisticated, context-aware systems we see today.

To provide readers with a comprehensive understanding, we will delve into the various technologies that enable Conversational AI. We will explain the concepts of Natural Language Processing and its branches, such as syntactic and semantic analysis, entity recognition, and sentiment analysis. Additionally, we will explore machine learning algorithms and frameworks that empower Conversational AI systems to learn from data and improve their performance based on user interactions.

Throughout the chapter, we will emphasize the importance of data in training and fine-tuning Conversational AI systems. We will discuss the challenges of data collection, data labeling, and the need for diverse and representative datasets to avoid biases and ensure inclusivity in Conversational AI applications.

Furthermore, this chapter will shed light on the applications of Conversational AI in different sectors. We will unveil how virtual assistants have become an integral part of our daily lives, assisting us with tasks such as scheduling appointments, providing weather updates, and answering general knowledge queries. We will also dive into the world of customer service chatbots, which have revolutionized customer support by providing instant responses and personalized assistance.

Readers will have gained a solid understanding of Conversational AI and its underlying technologies. They will appreciate the historical context and evolution of Conversational AI, comprehend the importance of Natural Language Processing, machine learning, and data in building efficient systems, and recognize the diverse applications of Conversational AI across multiple industries.

Through this introductory chapter, readers will have acquired the foundation they need to delve deeper into the subsequent chapters of the book, where we will explore advanced concepts, implementation strategies, and discuss the ethical considerations surrounding Conversational AI.

1.1 Evolution of Chatbots and Conversational AI

In recent years, there has been a noteworthy rise in the use of chatbots and conversational AI technology in various industries and sectors. From customer service to sales and marketing, these intelligent systems are revolutionizing how organizations communicate and interact with their audiences. If you are fascinated by the potential of chatbots and want to explore their journey of evolution, this book is the perfect guide for you.

Understanding the Evolution

Predecessors: Early Forms of Interactive Software

Let's delve into the beginnings of conversational technology to understand its lineage and early influential platforms like ELIZA, that marked the starting point of our journey. Analysis of its limitations and accomplishments forms the grounds to glean information for designing advanced chatbots in future.

Rule-Based Chatbots: Simple Solutions for Structured Queries

With advancements in computer science, hierarchical ontological domains, an infusion of expert systems and IF-THEN logic contributed toward the birth of rule-based chatbots. This section emphasizes their applicability for simple, well-structured conversations, elaborate on conversational authoring languages and tools accompanied through demonstrations for better grasp.

AI Development: Shaping Conversational Bot Capacities

Dive deep into the emergence of artificial intelligence (AI) and natural language processing (NLP) frameworks. We will explore the facets of machine learning and ways they have fundamentally reshaped the design and functionality of conversational AI systems.

Messaging Applications: Pioneers of Conversational Interfaces

Develop insights into messaging platforms that significantly influenced labs to make critical research developments. Learning about trends that brought chatbots into the web-mainstream, along with detailed explanations allied with design suggestions may prompt readers in-empaths spaghetti stories of earlier design aesthetics.

Messaging Interface-Driven Assistants: Setting the Standard

Explore advancements in modern user interfaces like Facebook Messenger, Slack, WhatsApp, and WeChat and API-driven innovations disintegrating bottlenecks of vertically pondering aims of adjoining to encapsulate success services/MOD.

1.2 Introduction to GPT (Generative Pre-trained Transformer)

There has been a paradigm shift in the field of Natural Language Processing (NLP) and machine learning, empowering computers to understand and generate human-like text. One of the most pioneering achievements in this domain is the emergence of the Generative Pre-trained Transformer (GPT).

GPT, developed by OpenAI, represents a groundbreaking advancement in language generation models. By utilizing advanced deep learning techniques and robust transformers, GPT is poised to revolutionize the way we decipher, generate, and utilize textual information.

This comprehensive book is designed as an introductory guide to help beginners navigate the complexities of understanding and implementing GPT in their NLP endeavors. Aimed at both aspiring and experienced researchers, software engineers, data scientists, and students interested in machine learning, this book will serve as your informative companion on the remarkable journey into the world of GPT.

Our exploration begins by introducing the fundamental concepts wielded by GPT. Grasping these concepts is essential to comprehend the inner workings of this highly revered language model. We'll walk you through the core technologies which underpin GPT fueled advancement in NLP, such as artificial neural networks, transformer architectures, and the promises of unsupervised learning.

With a solid understanding of these foundations, you'll then delve into the intricate details of how GPT assimilates, processes and generates text. We'll uncover the key building blocks comprising the GPT architecture, including the Encoder-Decoder model, attention mechanisms, and positional encoding—each playing a unique and pivotal role in the overall functioning of GPT.

Transitioning beyond theory, we enter the captivating realm of GPT applications. Together, we'll explore a wide range of GPT use cases, witnessing firsthand how this remarkable technology empowers compilers, enables code completion systems, boosts chatbot capabilities, aids in content generation, revolutionizes customer support, bolsters machine translation, maximizes summarization efficiency, shapes conversational agents, and transforms many other aspects of human-computer interaction.

As we embark on the journey of understanding GPT intricacies, we must also recognize its broader societal and ethical implications. With immense power comes tremendous responsibility. In recognition of this crucial aspect, we dedicates ample space in illuminating the ethical considerations and project guidance to ensure fair and unbiased use of GPT-powered models, eradicating risks such as comme AI system usage disinformation, biases, or infringement of privacy and safety.

This extensive and detailed book is unconstrained by novices alone. Recognizing the varying depths of knowledge readers may have, we have cleverly interspersed the chapters with trackable necessary introductory topics, abundant references, practical usage samples, and helpful tangential notes to ambitiously cater to both the earnest novice learner and the seasoned professional utilizing GPT already.

Irrespective of your expertise, our collective goal is to foster an understanding, a sense of empowerment, and unleash in the reader a spirit of innovation, leading to the prosperous integration and broader exploitation of this remarkable breakthrough generously offered by GPT.

As you embark upon the intricacies of GPT, I kindly provoke and exhilarate you not solely to enjoy the content of this book passively, but rather to seize this opportunity to unearth that vivid curiosity cultivated within—an unbounded source of drive that could usher substantial contributions to the never-ending realm of NLP, AI Monomorphism and transform your world while shaping our future as well. Get ready for a transformative experience, let the journey commence!

1.3 Overview of GPT-4 Chat – Newest Conversational AI Model

In this fast-paced era of technology, artificial intelligence (AI) continues to evolve and revolutionize various domains, bringing unprecedented advancements to our digital world. Specifically, conversational AI has gained significant attention due to its potential to enhance human-computer interactions, making machines more efficient and responsive in understanding and generating natural language. In this book, we delve into the fascinating realm of AI research to provide beginners with a comprehensive understanding of GPT-4 Chat – the newest conversational AI model.

Core Concepts:
To properly grasp the intricacies of GPT-4 Chat, it is crucial to garner a fundamental understanding of AI, language models, and conversational agents. We explain these concepts in simpler terms for beginners without compromising on the technical aspects. It is our goal to enable readers to comprehend the foundation upon which GPT-4 Chat is built; therefore, we dive into detail not only regarding neural networks but also the underlying components driving conversational AI.

Evolution of Conversational AI:
Before diving into discussing GPT-4 Chat, we take you on a journey through the evolution of conversational AI models, including their inception, incremental advancements, and

notable milestones. This historical perspective serves as a useful backdrop to understand the paradigm shifts that have led to the creation of GPT-4 Chat. You will gain insights into challenges faced, lessons learned, and breakthrough innovations that have paved the way for more sophisticated conversational agents.

Introducing GPT-4 Chat:
With a firm conceptual foundation in place, we delve into GPT-4 Chat – the latest addition to the renowned family of GPT models. Right from its introduction, we dissect GPT-4 Chat's architectural advancements, focusing on novel implementation strategies such as dense reasoning, adaptive plugging, and enhanced transfer learning techniques. Employing relatable examples and analogies, we demystify the technical nuances behind these enhancements, allowing readers from non-technical backgrounds to grasp their significance seamlessly.

Training and Fine-tuning the Model:
Models like GPT-4 Chat require attention and meticulous training to ensure optimal performance. We shed light on the training methodologies employed, such as unsupervised learning and reinforcement learning, as well as

how fine-tuning is done to cater the model for various use cases. Understanding the intricate training aspects gives readers solid grasp of how the model is shaped and refined, enabling them to appreciate its capabilities further.

Impact on Industries:
Finally, we take a step back to contemplate the remarkable impact that GPT-4 Chat has on various industries. It is crucial to explore how conversational AI models can be utilized in real-world applications, from customer support to healthcare. By examining implementation case studies, discovery of potential challenges, and mitigation strategies, we present an unbiased analysis of GPT-4 Chat's potential while striving to forecast its future contribution to revolutionizing human-machine interactions.

Readers will have comprehensive insights into the foundations, enhancements, and impact of GPT-4 Chat – the newest conversational AI model. Armed with this knowledge, readers can approach subsequent chapters with confidence, ready to explore the intricacies of GPT-4 Chat and unravel the mysteries of this powerful conversational AI technology. So, fasten your seatbelts, as we embark together on this enlightening journey through the awe-inspiring world of GPT-4 Chat!

1.4 The Potential and Real-World Applications of GPT-4 Chat

Artificial Intelligence (AI) has rapidly gained prominence in recent years, revolutionizing various aspects of our lives. In particular, natural language processing (NLP) has witnessed remarkable advancements with the emergence of transformer-based models. One such groundbreaking model is GPT-4 Chat.

GPT-4 Chat, the fourth iteration of OpenAI's Generative Pre-trained Transformer (GPT) series, brings forth an array of astonishing capabilities that have the potential to qualitatively transform human-computer interactions. In this book, we will explore the multifarious applications and delve into the immense potential GPT-4 Chat holds for various real-world scenarios.

As an AI research expert, I aim to demystify the fascinating world of GPT-4 Chat for beginners, providing an in-depth understanding of its underlying technology and exploring its wide-ranging applications. Throughout this book, we will embark on a comprehensive journey that will equip readers with a solid foundation to comprehend and appreciate this incredible technology.

From enhancing virtual assistants and customer service platforms to augmenting educational experiences, GPT-4 Chat takes conversational AI to uncharted territories. Whether you are a software developer, a language processing enthusiast, or simply curious about the immense potential of AI, this book will give you a comprehensive view of the real-world applications GPT-4 Chat can offer.

Together, we will unravel the inner workings of GPT-4 Chat, comprehending the underlying mechanisms that power its fluent conversation generation and its ability to mimic human-like responses. We will explore not only its strengths but also the limitations associated with its deployment in various real-world contexts, thus enabling readers to make informed decisions about the feasibility of integrating GPT-4 Chat into their applications.

Throughout the chapters, we will dive into a myriad of contexts where GPT-4 Chat excels. We will delve into how GPT-4 Chat can augment ecommerce experiences, transform the healthcare industry through virtual symptom analysis, and provide personalized language learning assistance. We will explore how it can revolutionize customer support interactions, bolster content generation mechanisms, and enhance dialogue systems.

Additionally, ethical considerations associated with GPT-4 Chat will be discussed extensively. We will examine issues, such as bias and fairness, privacy concerns, and risks of malicious actors exploiting the tool. By highlighting potential challenges, we can pave the way for responsible development and integration of GPT-4 Chat in the real-world ecosystem.

As a reader, you will accompany me on a captivating journey, uncovering the potential and real-world applications of GPT-4 Chat. By the end of this book, you will possess a comprehensive understanding of this game-changing conversational AI tool and be equipped to leverage its transformative capabilities.

So, without further ado, let us delve into the astounding possibilities that lie within the realm of GPT-4 Chat. Join me as we embark on a quest to unveil its potential and unlock the doors to a future where artificial intelligence converses seamlessly with humans, profoundly shaping the way we perceive and interact with technology.

Part I: Getting Started with GPT-4 Chat

2. Setting up your Environment

2.1 Hardware and Software Requirements

In today's digital age, understanding the fundamentals of computer hardware and software has become increasingly essential. Whether you are a curious beginner or aspire to pursue a career in the field of technology, this book is designed to provide you with a comprehensive understanding of the hardware and software components that power our digital world.

The Importance of Hardware and Software Requirements

The Significance of Hardware Requirements:
Computers consist of a multitude of interconnected physical components that work together to execute tasks efficiently. Understanding hardware requirements is crucial

as it enables users to make informed decisions when purchasing or upgrading their machines. By gauging the capabilities and limitations of computer hardware, users can ensure optimal performance and avoid compatibility issues.

The Essence of Software Requirements:
Software acts as the bridge between users and their computers, allowing them to perform numerous tasks and operations. Recognizing software requirements allows individuals to choose the right applications and programs that align with their needs. Moreover, comprehending software compatibility is necessary to prevent conflicts and ensure smooth functioning of the computer system.

Hardware Requirements
Central Processing Unit (CPU):
The CPU serves as the brain of the computer, performing calculations, executing instructions, and managing the overall operation of the system. This section explores the different types of CPUs, their architectures, clock speeds, and the factors influencing their performance.

Random Access Memory (RAM):

RAM facilitates the temporary storage of data and instructions that the CPU needs for immediate processing. Understanding RAM capacities, types, and access speeds helps users choose the optimal amount and configuration to suit their computing requirements.

Storage Devices:
Storage devices play a crucial role in retaining data even when the computer is powered off. This section delves into various types of storage devices, such as hard disk drives (HDDs), solid-state drives (SSDs), and hybrid drives. It also discusses their capacity, speed, reliability, and factors to consider when selecting an appropriate storage solution.

Graphics Processing Unit (GPU):
GPUs are specialized processors designed to handle complex graphical computations, making them essential for multimedia tasks, gaming, and parallel processing. This section explores the different types of GPUs, their architectures, and the factors influencing their performance.

Software Requirements
Operating Systems (OS):

The operating system acts as an interface between users and the computer hardware, allowing them to interact with various software applications. This section provides insights into different OS types (e.g., Windows, macOS, Linux) and their functionalities, system requirements, and compatibility with different hardware components.

Application Software:
Application software includes a wide range of programs tailored to perform specific tasks or cater to specific user needs. This section discusses various software categories, such as productivity tools, graphic design software, video editors, and gaming applications. It also emphasizes the importance of considering software requirements before installing or purchasing applications.

Drivers and Firmware:
Drivers and firmware are essential components that enable communication between hardware devices and the operating system. Understanding the need for up-to-date drivers and firmware helps ensure compatibility, enhances performance, and addresses security vulnerabilities.

By delving into the intricate worlds of hardware and software requirements, this chapter lays the foundation for a deeper comprehension of the functioning and optimization of computer systems. Armed with this knowledge, readers can make informed decisions when purchasing, upgrading, or troubleshooting their computers, enabling them to unleash the full potential of technology in their professional and personal lives.

2.2 Installation and Configuration Steps

Installing and configuring software is an integral part of any computer-related task, and in the realm of Artificial Intelligence (AI), it becomes even more crucial. This chapter will guide you through an in-depth exploration of the installation and configuration steps required to set up a robust AI environment.

Before delving into the details, it is essential to mention that AI encompasses a vast landscape of concepts, techniques, and applications. Therefore, there is no single software package that will cater to all your AI needs right out of the box. Instead, AI environments are built by integrating multiple libraries, frameworks, and tools offering specialized functionalities.

The first step towards setting up an AI environment is to choose an appropriate programming language. Python, due to its versatility, extensive community support, and availability of several AI-specific libraries, has emerged as the de facto language for AI development. Therefore, this book predominantly focuses on Python-based installations and configurations.

To get started, it is crucial to have an understanding of the Python ecosystem and the various AI dependencies that can transform it into a powerful tool for building AI models and applications. Most notably, we need to discuss two significant components – Python distributions and package managers.

Python distributions, such as Anaconda and Miniconda, provide everything you need for a full-fledged Python environment specifically tailored for scientific computing and AI development. These distributions package not only Python itself but also popular AI libraries like NumPy, pandas, and TensorFlow. We'll walk you through the installation process for both Anaconda and Miniconda, and explain the differences between them, empowering you to make an informed choice.

Package managers like pip and conda play a pivotal role in managing and installing additional Python libraries beyond what the distributions provide. A breadth of AI-specific libraries can be effortlessly installed using these package managers, empowering you to leverage cutting-edge functionalities from various sources effortlessly. We'll guide you through the installation of both pip and conda and discuss their respective usage scenarios.

Next, we'll dive into the installation and configuration of some essential AI libraries and frameworks, including TensorFlow, PyTorch, and scikit-learn, which constitute the backbone of AI development. These libraries offer powerful and flexible tools for tasks such as building neural networks, training machine learning models, and implementing data preprocessing techniques. We'll thoroughly explore the installation procedures for each of them, highlighting any potential pitfalls you might encounter during the process.

As AI environments usually require a substantial amount of computational power, we explore how to harness the benefits of Graphics Processing Units (GPUs) to accelerate AI computations. We'll provide insights into the installation and configuration of GPU drivers, CUDA, and cuDNN, enabling you to accelerate your AI workloads and achieve significant speedups.

Finally, to ensure reproducibility and ease of collaboration in AI projects, we look into the concept of virtual environments. These isolated software contexts allow you to separate the dependencies of each project, ensuring that software updates or conflicts in one project do not affect others. We'll guide you through the installation and setup of virtual environment managers like virtualenv and conda environments, empowering you to manage your AI projects with efficiency and ease.

By the end of this chapter, you will have acquired a comprehensive understanding of the crucial installation and configuration steps required to establish a versatile AI environment. Armed with this knowledge, you can confidently proceed to explore the wide-ranging possibilities and intricacies that the vast field of AI offers. Let's dive into these steps, allowing you to elevate your AI endeavors to new heights!

2.3 Familiarizing with the GPT-4 Chat Interface
The GPT-4 Chat Interface is a powerful tool that allows users to interact with the state-of-the-art GPT-4 model in order to build conversational AI applications. In this section, we will explore the workings of the GPT-4 Chat Interface and how to utilize its capabilities effectively.

Upon opening the GPT-4 Chat Interface, you will be greeted with a simple and intuitive user interface. The interface consists of a text input field where queries or prompts can be entered, and a chat window that displays the responses generated by the GPT-4 model.

To use the interface effectively, it is essential to understand the principles behind the prompts provided to GPT-4. Prompts act as textual instructions that guide the model to generate the desired output. It's important to frame prompts in a way that prompts accurate and helpful responses from the model.

A basic prompt can be as simple as a single sentence, such as "Tell me a joke." However, GPT-4 can process more complex prompts, including providing moment-to-moment instructions during a conversation, asking multiple questions, or presenting context.

The GPT-4 model itself has been trained on a massive corpus of text data, enabling it to generate impressive responses across a wide range of topics. Despite its remarkable abilities, GPT-4 might have limitations or biases rooted in the data it was trained on. It is important to approach the model with an understanding of its capabilities and constraints.

When engaging in a conversation with GPT-4, it is helpful to keep in mind that the model generates responses based on the information it receives in prompts. Therefore, asking specific and detailed questions or providing clear context can greatly enhance the quality of the responses. On the other hand, vague or ambiguous prompts might lead to less accurate or less helpful responses.

Additionally, GPT-4 responds to whatever is visible in the conversation history. This means that the entire conversation up until that point influences GPT-4's response. Therefore, maintaining a clear and coherent conversation history is vital to ensure accurate and contextual replies.

The GPT-4 Chat Interface offers several additional features and options to enhance your conversational AI experience. For instance, you can customize the system prompt, which is a message that is internally constructed by the interface to introduce the model to conversation and can significantly influence the responses generated. Carefully crafting a suitable system prompt can guide the model's behavior in the desired direction.

It is important to understand that GPT-4 should be used responsibly and ethically. Due to its ability to generate human-like responses, it can be used to spread misinformation or promote harmful content if not handled diligently. Being mindful of these ethical considerations and using the tool responsibly will help harness the power of GPT-4 in a positive and constructive manner.

The GPT-4 Chat Interface is a user-friendly tool that allows individuals to engage with GPT-4, an advanced conversational AI model. Familiarizing yourself with the workings of the chat interface, understanding how prompts influence responses, and utilizing additional features responsibly will enable you to harness the potential of GPT-4 effectively for your conversational AI projects.

3. Navigating the GPT-4 Chat Interface
3.1 Exploring the User Interface Components

In this digital era, user interfaces govern the way we interact with various technological devices, from personal computers to mobile phones, and even sophisticated machinery. A powerful user interface provides us with an intuitive and efficient means to communicate with machines, seamlessly bridging the gap between humans and technology.

Understanding the fundamental components that constitute user interfaces is pivotal in building visually appealing and user-friendly designs. As we embark on this exploration of user interface components, you will gain insights into the building blocks that form the foundation of modern interfaces. With this knowledge, you will acquire practical skills to craft interfaces that are both aesthetically pleasing and highly functional.

One of the essential components of any user interface is buttons. Often regarded as the core interactive element, buttons enable users to perform specific actions or trigger events. Properly designed buttons grab users' attention, carry out their desired functions, and provide a visual effect indicating interactivity. By mastering the art of button design, you can empower users to control and manipulate elements of an interface effortlessly.

Another crucial aspect is the Input Box or Input Field, which empowers users to enter or modify text-based information. Input fields appear in forms, message boxes, search bars, and various other contexts, empowering users to provide input or receive data. Understanding the characteristics of input boxes, such as size, validation, formatting, and suggestions, enables us to design interfaces that encourage accurate and efficient data entry.

Scrollbars allow users to navigate content which is too large or not fully displayed on the screen. As the name suggests, these elements help in scrolling or panning through content by moving vertically or horizontally. An effective scrollbar design should indicate the current position, indicate the size of content, and facilitate smooth navigation with minimal effort.

Navigational elements, such as menus, provide users with a hierarchical path, enabling them to explore an interface, jump to different sections, and perform specific actions with ease. Understanding the nuances of menu design, including menu types, hierarchical structure, selection cues, and accessibility, allows us to create intuitive navigation experiences reducing user frustration and improving efficiency.

Progress indicators or progress bars spin or fill gradually to visually indicate the progress of an ongoing task. These nifty UI components keep users informed about the status of time-consuming operations and prevent the feeling of uncertainty or lack of control. Designing progress indicators intelligently, using appropriate animations, and providing relevant status updates is essential for instilling confidence and ensuring a positive user experience.

Lastly, radio buttons and checkboxes play a significant role when users need to select one or more options from a set of mutually exclusive or non-exclusive alternatives, respectively.

Harnessing the power of radio buttons and checkboxes facilitates concise data input and selection mechanisms necessary for collecting and filtering information appropriately.

To become proficient in developing captivating user interfaces, mastering the intricacies of these various components is essential. This chapter delves extensively into the design considerations, usability principles, and best practices associated with each user interface component discussed above. Expanding your knowledge in this domain will empower you to create interfaces that are not only visually stimulating but also enhance the overall user experience.

So, let's not waste any more time and dive straight into the exciting world of exploring user interface components to unlock the true potential of your user interface designs!

3.2 Understanding the Input and Output Format
In the ever-evolving field of Artificial Intelligence (AI), understanding the input and output format is essential for any aspiring AI enthusiast or practitioner. Whether you are just starting your journey into the world of AI or are already familiar with the concepts, comprehending the intricacies

of input and output formats is fundamental to building efficient and effective AI models.

To grasp the concept of input and output format, let's first delve into what they entail. In the context of AI, the input format refers to the way data is presented to an AI model for processing. This can vary depending on the specific AI task at hand. For example, in image recognition tasks, the input format might consist of images, whereas in natural language processing, it could be textual data. These formats are often diverse and complex, necessitating a comprehensive understanding to successfully work with AI models.

Understanding the input format involves considering various factors. Firstly, it is crucial to comprehend the structure and representation of data. Images may be represented as pixel intensities in a matrix, audio data as a series of amplitudes, and text data as a sequence of words or characters. Recognizing these representations and their peculiarities is key to extracting meaningful insights from the data. Additionally, understanding the range, scale, and distribution of the data aids in preprocessing and normalization, which are vital for effective AI model training.

Moreover, exploring the input format requires familiarity with preprocessing techniques. Raw data may seldom be in a suitable format for direct consumption by AI models. Preprocessing steps such as data cleaning, dimensionality reduction, and feature extraction help transform the input into a format that the AI model can efficiently comprehend. These preprocessing techniques typically involve statistical methods, signal processing algorithms, or linguistic tools, depending on the nature of the data. Mastering these techniques empowers AI practitioners to optimize model performance and enhance overall accuracy.

Understanding the output format forms the other side of the coin. It pertains to how the AI model presents the results after processing the input data. Similar to input formats, output formats also vary depending on the task. It could range from predicting numeric values to classifying images into distinct categories or generating natural language text. Each output format has its particular nuances, which necessitates keen attention to detail and a solid understanding of the task requirements.

For effective analysis and interpretation of AI model outputs, it is essential to comprehend error metrics and evaluation methods. Different AI tasks demand different evaluation techniques. Evaluating image recognition models may involve metrics such as accuracy, precision, and recall, while evaluating language translation models may focus on measures like BLEU score or perplexity. Awareness of these evaluation techniques empowers AI practitioners to assess model performance, troubleshoot potential issues, and iterate to enhance accuracy continually.

To succeed in the AI field, mastering the input and output format is vital. It enables AI practitioners to navigate through the complexities of data representation, preprocessing, and evaluation, thereby creating models that achieve impactful and reliable results. By honing their understanding of input and output formats, beginners and experts alike can unlock the true potential of AI and contribute to the advancement of this intriguing field.

3.3 Accessing Advanced Settings and Options

Technology has become an integral part of our daily lives. From smartphones to laptops and smart home devices, we rely on technology to stay connected, informed, and productive. However, while many of these devices come with default settings that cater to the average user, there are often advanced settings and options that can enhance the user experience and unlock exciting features. In Chapter 3, we delve into the realm of advanced settings and options, providing you with the knowledge and skills necessary to access and utilize these powerful tools.

Accessing the advanced settings and options of your devices and applications can greatly expand your capabilities and customization options. Whether you are a tech enthusiast eager to explore new features or a beginner seeking to optimize your device's performance, this chapter is designed to equip you with the essential techniques and strategies to navigate advanced settings with ease.

As you embark on this journey, it is important to understand that advanced settings and options can vary significantly across different devices, operating systems, and applications. Therefore, this chapter provides a general framework that can be applied universally, while offering specific examples and step-by-step instructions for popular devices and applications. By following these guidelines, you will be able to adapt the methods to suit your own specific device or software.

To begin, we introduce you to the concept of advanced settings and options, explaining their significance and the potential benefits of exploring them. We highlight how these settings can help personalize your experience by allowing you to tailor the device or application to your unique preferences. Moreover, we emphasize the advantages of accessing advanced settings, such as improved performance, privacy, and security.

Next, we discuss the common methods of accessing advanced settings and options on different platforms. This includes navigating system settings on operating systems like Windows, macOS, iOS, and Android, as well as accessing application-specific settings on popular applications such as Microsoft Office, Adobe Creative Suite, and web browsers. We provide detailed instructions and screenshots to ensure a smooth and effortless process for readers at any level of technical proficiency.

Furthermore, this chapter addresses some key considerations to keep in mind when exploring advanced settings and options. We emphasize the importance of understanding the implications of each setting change, as well as caution against making unnecessary modifications that may compromise the stability or functionality of your device. We encourage readers to exercise caution and patience, recommending that they carefully read through the documentation or seek expert advice when unsure.

To aid your understanding and ensure a comprehensive learning experience, we include case studies and practical examples throughout the chapter. These illustrate how accessing advanced settings and options can be beneficial in various scenarios, such as improving battery life on a smartphone, customizing keyboard shortcuts on a computer, or enhancing the privacy settings of your favorite social media application.

You will have gained the necessary knowledge and skills to confidently access advanced settings and options on your devices and applications. You will be equipped with the tools to personalize your digital experience and harness the full potential of your technology. So, let us embark on this exciting journey together, as we unravel the world of advanced settings and options that awaits you.

3.4 Interacting with the Model via API

We will dive into the fascinating world of application programming interfaces, commonly known as APIs. In recent years, APIs have gained enormous popularity and are regarded as the fundamental building blocks for enabling interaction between different software systems.

Understanding APIs

Before we explore how to interact with AI models using APIs, let's take a moment to understand what APIs are. An API can be described as a contract between two pieces of software, defining the capabilities and rules for communication. Simply put, it allows one software application to speak to and utilize the functionalities of another.

APIs come in different forms but often rely on well-defined protocols, standards, or frameworks. These essential structures define the inputs, outputs, and endpoints through which systems can engage with each other. Whether it's accessing weather information from an online service, posting a tweet using a social media platform, or even asking a digital assistant for directions, behind these activities lies the immense power of APIs.

Interacting with AI Models

As we progress deeper into the realm of AI technologies, interacting with AI models becomes incredibly valuable. APIs enable third-party developers, researchers, and businesses to enhance their applications by leveraging cutting-edge AI capabilities effortlessly. Thanks to APIs, these models are no longer confined within proprietary software but are accessible to a broader audience, leading to immense growth and innovation.

To interact with AI models using APIs, the model's creators typically expose specific endpoints that define the available functions and allow external systems to make requests. This request-response mechanism forms the core of most AI model APIs. It enables a seamless flow of information between your application and the model, leveraging its predictive or generative capabilities in real-time.

When interacting with an AI model via API, you should keep a few key considerations in mind. Firstly, ensure proper authentication and authorization controls are in place. These security measures safeguard the model's data and prevent any unauthorized access. Secondly, familiarize yourself with the API documentation provided by the model's creator. It contains vital information about the endpoint functionalities, required inputs, expected outputs, and any additional parameters or constraints.

Upon understanding the API's functionalities and requirements, you can begin sending requests to make predictions or generate outputs using the AI model. Generally, these requests must include the specific input data with which you want the model to work. The data could be in the form of textual prompts, images, audio clips, or any other format relevant to the specific application domain. By utilizing these inputs as prescribed by the API, you can harness the power of AI to obtain valuable and insightful results.

It is worth mentioning that different AI models might expose various nuances of interaction via API. Some models request additional parameters or details in the request payload, such as the desired temperature for text generation models or the maximum length of output sequences. Exploring the API documentation crucially ensures you optimize your interaction with the model, discovering the full range of possibilities and extracting the maximum utility.

Best Practices for Interacting with AI Models via API

To ensure a seamless and efficient experience while interacting with AI models via APIs, it is beneficial to follow some best practices. These practices not only streamline your integration efforts but also enhance the robustness and reliability of your applications. Here are some key recommendations to consider:

Familiarize yourself with the API documentation: The API documentation provided by the model's creators acts as a valuable guide to understand the available functionalities, inputs, and outputs. Spending time to thoroughly explore and comprehend this documentation significantly contributes to leveraging the full potential of the AI model.

Implement proper error handling: API interactions can encounter errors due to various reasons – from invalid inputs to network connection issues. To gracefully handle errors, it is essential to implement proper error handling mechanisms into your application. This allows your application to respond accordingly and mitigate any potential disruption caused by API-related issues.

Carefully manage API rate limits: Many AI model APIs impose rate limits to ensure fair usage of system resources. It is essential to understand the specific rate limits set by the API you are interacting with and make adjustments within your own application to stay within these limits. Overstepping the defined boundaries may lead to usage restrictions or deteriorated performance.

Optimize data preparation and preprocessing: Adequately preparing and preprocessing your input data before making API requests significantly impacts the model's performance and the quality of results. Investing time in data preparation, including correct formatting, cleaning, and normalization, can enhance the model's ability to provide accurate and useful predictions.

Leverage batching for improved efficiency: Where possible and applicable, consider optimizing your API interactions by sending batches of input data rather than individual requests. Batching reduces the overall execution time and minimizes redundant communication overhead. However, ensure you balance batch size for optimal performance, as excessively large batches could impede response times.

Implementing these best practices not only ensures smooth integration of AI models into your applications, but also fosters a reliable, efficient, and intelligent software ecosystem for users to benefit from.

Understanding how to interact with AI models through APIs opens up endless possibilities for harnessing the power of AI technology. This chapter guided you through the significance of APIs, outlined the key considerations for interacting with AI models via API, and highlighted some best practices to facilitate your integration efforts. By leveraging API-empowered AI models, you can augment your application's capabilities, enhance user experiences, and delve into transformative innovations.

The exploration and utilization of AI technology results from collaboration and knowledge sharing, continually striving for advancements and making AI accessible to wider audiences. By mastering the art of interacting with AI models via API, your integration endeavors become a stepping stone towards an intelligent and interconnected digital future.

Part II: Leveraging GPT-4 Chat Capabilities

4. Preparing High-Quality Input
4.1 Crafting Contextual Prompts for Effective Conversations

In today's advancing world full of artificial intelligence (AI) and chatbots, engaging in meaningful and human-like conversations with machines is becoming increasingly common. As humans, our natural ability to communicate is one that sets us apart from other species. It allows us to express our thoughts, feelings, and desires, facilitating the exchange of information and strengthening our relationships.

Although machines lack human emotions, they have made tremendous strides in replicating human-like conversational abilities through machine learning and natural language processing techniques. These advancements have sparked a profound interest in creating AI models that can effectively interact with users in various domains, from customer support to personal assistance.

However, generating natural and context-aware responses remains one of the key challenges in Conversational AI. Context plays a vital role in any conversation, as it provides meaning, guidance, and relevance to what is being communicated. Humans instinctively utilize contextual cues to perceive, interpret, and respond to their surroundings, making conversation more natural, smooth, and effective.

We delve into the art of crafting contextual prompts for generating effective conversations, which enable AI models to understand and respond appropriately in a given context. We explore various strategies and techniques employed in the development of AI models that demonstrate contextual intelligence.

Understanding Context:
Before exploring the craft of creating contextual prompts, it is crucial to understand the concept of context itself. Context encompasses a wide range of elements such as the current conversation history, the underlying user intent, and the surrounding environment.
Contextual prompts essentially provide relevant cues and signals that guide the AI model's response generation process. Despite possessing massive neural networks and powerful computational abilities, AI models still require carefully crafted prompts to generate meaningful and contextually appropriate responses.

Crafting Contextually Appropriate Prompts:
To improve the conversation quality of AI models, crafting contextually appropriate prompts is of paramount importance. It requires a systematic approach that considers the unique characteristics of the conversational domain and the specific requirements of users.

Utilizing Historical Dialogues:
Leveraging prior conversations (called dialogue history) is a fundamental aspect of enhancing contextual understanding. By providing AI models with previous interactions, they can effectively comprehend the ongoing conversation and respond accurately. Crafting prompts that incorporate relevant snippets from dialogue history can significantly contribute to the contextual awareness of AI models.

Incorporating User's Intent:
Understanding user intent is key to engaging in meaningful conversations. AI models should be able to discern the user's needs, aspirations, or objective behind a given dialogue. By incorporating prompts that capture the user's intent, the model becomes capable of generating prompt-aware responses that address the precise inquiries or requirements expressed by the user.

Seamlessly Handling Context Switches:
Conversations often involve changing topics or moving between subtasks. AI models need to gracefully navigate these transitions and maintain an appropriate understanding of context throughout the entire conversation. Crafting

prompts that facilitate smooth context switches is crucial in creating conversational agents that can handle diverse user requirements effortlessly.

Encoding Prior Knowledge:
Incorporating external knowledge sources, such as encyclopedic data or pre-trained models, is essential for AI models to possess sufficient domain expertise and generate contextually appropriate responses. Prompts should be designed to encourage the utilization of prior knowledge in generating well-informed and accurate replies.

Crafting contextually aware prompts is a crucial step towards building AI models that can engage in truly effective conversations. It enables AI models to comprehend, interpret, and respond based on their understanding of the conversational context. By meticulously designing prompts that capture historical dialogues, user intent, seamless context switching, and prior knowledge, we can empower AI models to converse naturally like humans do. In the subsequent sections of this book, we will explore in greater detail the techniques, methodologies, and innovations available to create contextually intelligent conversational agents.

4.2 Utilizing System and User Messages

As we delve deeper into the fascinating world of Artificial Intelligence (AI), it becomes apparent that creating engaging and interactive AI systems requires a deep understanding of how to effectively communicate with users. In this section, we will explore the nuances and strategies involved in utilizing system and user messages, aiming to enhance the overall user experience.

In the realm of AI, system and user messages play a crucial role in conveying information and eliciting responses from users. These messages act as a bridge of communication, enabling developers to design AI systems that can guide, inform, and seek input from their users. To truly create immersive and user-friendly AI experiences, it is essential to leverage these messages effectively.

We will begin by understanding the distinct nature of system and user messages. We will explore their purposes, aiming to lay a solid foundation for comprehending their individual roles in AI systems.

Furthermore, we will delve into the key characteristics of effective system messages. We will discuss how to design and structure these messages in a manner that is concise, clear, and coherent. By grasping the art of crafting efficient system messages, beginners will be equipped to build AI systems that can effectively convey information and instructions to users.

Our exploration will then shift towards user messages, focusing on strategies for eliciting meaningful responses from users. We will explore various approaches, ranging from open-ended questioning to providing multiple-choice options, aiming to empower developers with a diverse toolkit to engage users effectively.

Furthermore, we will delve into the concept of error and alert messages. We will examine how to design error messages that are informative, helpful, and tactful in guiding users back on track. A deep understanding of creating useful error messages can prevent frustration and enhance the user's experience with the AI system.

As we progress through this section, we will also discuss best practices for optimizing system and user messages across different AI platforms. Understanding how to adapt messages for various mediums, such as chatbots, voice assistants, or mobile applications, will enable developers to create inclusive and versatile AI interactions.

Throughout this section, beginners will gain valuable insights into the fundamental principles underlying the effective utilization of system and user messages. By grasping the art of creating impactful and engaging AI interactions, developers will be poised to create user experiences that are both intuitive and engaging, fostering a positive relationship between humans and machines.

4.3 Incorporating Context from Past Conversations

Why context matters:
Imagine having a conversation with a friend who doesn't remember anything you previously discussed. It would be frustrating, right? The ability to reference past conversations enables the development of more human-like and

coherent dialogue systems. By incorporating context from past interactions, the AI model gains the ability to understand user preferences, maintain coherence, and deliver more accurate and relevant responses.

Types of context:
Contextual information in conversations can come in different forms, and it's essential to incorporate the relevant types to enhance the conversational experience. Let's explore some key aspects of context within conversations:

User context: Understanding the user's background, preferences, and behavior helps the conversational AI to tailor responses to their specific needs. For example, if a user inquires about the best Italian restaurants, the AI model can leverage their past conversations to recommend places according to their preferred cuisine preferences.

System context: The system context refers to the state of the conversational agent itself. It encapsulates information such as the current task, the dialogue history, and any partially completed actions. Incorporating the system context enables the conversational AI to generate relevant and coherent responses that align with the ongoing task or topic.

Dialogue context: The dialogue context encompasses the immediate conversational history between the user and the AI model. It includes the sequence of previous turns, each containing utterances from both the user and the AI system. By considering this dialogue context, the model can understand the flow of the conversation and generate appropriate responses that build upon prior exchanges.

Techniques for incorporating context:
Building context-aware conversational AI models involves the use of various techniques and approaches. Here, we explore a few prevalent methods:

Memory Networks: Memory Networks provide a way to explicitly store and retrieve information from past conversations. They allow the model to encode and access dialogue history efficiently, ensuring a knowledgeable and relevant response generation process.

Recurrent Neural Networks (RNNs): RNNs are neural networks that process sequential data, making them suitable for modeling conversational context. By employing recurrent connections, RNNs can retain information from past turns and automatically adapt their responses based on the dynamically changing conversation.

Attention Mechanisms: Attention mechanisms enable the model to focus on specific parts of the past conversation while generating responses. By attending to different dialogue elements, such as user queries or relevant system responses, the model can produce contextually appropriate replies.

Transformer Models: Transformer models, notably the Transformer architecture, revolutionized the field of Conversational AI. With their attention mechanisms and multi-head self-attention mechanisms, Transformers excel in capturing contextual dependencies across conversations, making them an effective choice for incorporating past context.

Challenges and considerations:
Incorporating context from past conversations is not without its challenges. Some key considerations include managing memory

limitations, addressing the ambiguity arising from long conversation histories, and handling situations where the context becomes irrelevant or outdated.

Moreover, privacy concerns play a crucial role when dealing with users' conversational history. Striking the right balance between personalization and privacy is of utmost importance when designing context-aware conversational AI systems.

We explored the significance of incorporating context from past conversations and overviewed the various types of context that contribute to building more engaging and personalized conversational agents. We discussed techniques such as Memory Networks, RNNs, attention mechanisms, and Transformer models that effectively capture and utilize conversation history.

Understanding how to incorporate context is vital for creating advanced conversational AI systems that possess better comprehension, coherence, and user-centricity. By learning from past interactions, these models can establish long-term memory, adapt responses based on user preferences, and facilitate more natural, engaging conversations.

4.4 Handling Sensitive Topics and Bias in Inputs
In the rapidly advancing field of artificial intelligence (AI), researchers and developers work relentlessly to create systems that can perform complex tasks, learn from data, and make decisions that emulate human intelligence. As AI technologies become increasingly integrated into various aspects of our lives, it is essential to address the challenges and considerations associated with handling sensitive topics and bias in inputs.

Sensitive topics refer to issues that are considered personal, controversial, or emotionally charged, such as race, gender, religion, and political affiliations. Bias, on the other hand, refers to the unintentional skew or favoritism in how AI systems process information, which can result in unfair outcomes or perpetuate existing societal inequalities. Both sensitive topics and bias require careful attention and proactive measures to ensure ethical AI development and deployment.

It is crucial to acknowledge that AI systems are trained using massive amounts of data, and the quality and diversity of that data play a significant role in shaping the behavior and decision-making capabilities of these systems. Unfortunately, biases that exist in society can permeate into the data used to train AI models, leading to systems that unwittingly reproduce and amplify those biases. For instance, if a particular dataset predominantly includes information that favors one group over another, the AI model trained on that data will inevitably adopt those biases and potentially discriminate against certain individuals or communities.

Understanding and addressing bias in AI requires a careful examination of the data used for training, as well as the algorithms and models employed. Researchers should meticulously evaluate the training datasets, looking for imbalances, underrepresentation, or overrepresentation of specific demographics, viewpoints, or perspectives. Identifying and mitigating biases requires a strong commitment to fairness, transparency, and diversity by actively involving individuals from various backgrounds and expertise during the development process.

Moreover, handling sensitive topics involves navigating ethical considerations with utmost care and empathy. When designing AI systems or developing AI-powered applications, it is crucial to anticipate and mitigate potential risks of harm or discrimination. Developers must ensure that AI algorithms do not make decisions that could infringe upon individual privacy, perpetuate harmful stereotypes, or violate ethical principles. Respecting user privacy, securing personal data, and establishing clear guidelines for the responsible use of AI in sensitive contexts are essential steps in preventing unintended consequences or misuse.

The responsibility to address these challenges does not lie solely with AI researchers and developers; it also extends to policymakers, organizations, and society as a whole. It is imperative for policymakers to establish legal frameworks, regulations, and guidelines that promote fairness, accountability, and transparency in AI systems. Organizations must foster a culture that values diversity, inclusion, and ethics, committing to ongoing education and training for employees involved in AI development. Society at large should engage in discussions, debates, and critical reflections on the implications and impact of AI technologies to ensure their equitable and ethical use.

In the forthcoming chapters of this book, we will delve further into the various strategies and techniques for handling sensitive topics and reducing bias in AI systems. We will explore methodologies for detecting and mitigating bias during data collection, preprocessing, and model training. Additionally, we will discuss approaches to designing fair and robust algorithms that can handle sensitive inputs without perpetuating stereotypes or harmful biases. By doing so, we aim to equip beginners in the field of AI with the knowledge and tools necessary to develop responsible and unbiased AI applications. Stay tuned for an insightful and transformative journey ahead in this exciting field!

5. Navigating GPT-4 Chat Responses

5.1 Analyzing GPT-4 Chat Output Structure

GPT-4, the fourth iteration of the Generative Pre-trained Transformer model, has revolutionized natural language processing, enabling sophisticated conversational abilities. It has undeniably improved upon its predecessors, incorporating enhanced capabilities and achieving impressive levels of fluency and coherence. However, understanding the structure of its chat outputs can be a complex task, as the model operates on a vast amount of data and employs intricate algorithms to generate responses.

Analyzing the structure of GPT-4 chat outputs provides valuable insights into how the model comprehends and generates human-like conversations. Through this analysis, we can gain a deeper understanding of the underlying mechanisms that drive its responses, allowing us to make informed observations and uncover potential strengths and limitations of the model.

One fundamental aspect to consider when examining GPT-4's chat output structure is its ability to maintain context. The model remains coherent throughout a conversation, recalling previous messages and incorporating them into its responses. This contextual understanding greatly enhances the natural flow of conversation and distinguishes GPT-4 from previous iterations.

Furthermore, GPT-4 demonstrates a remarkable ability to generate diverse and creative responses. It can generate text that aligns with a wide range of conversational styles, exhibiting nuances, humor, and empathy. Understanding how GPT-4 accomplishes this level of sophistication is key to appreciating its abilities fully.

In addition to the overall structure, it is essential to focus on understanding GPT-4's sentence structuring and coherence. GPT-4's responses are crafted with the intention of sounding human-like. The model employs tactics such as utilizing appropriate grammar and syntax, employing relevant vocabulary, and maintaining logical and coherent discourse. Analyzing the sentence structure within its chat outputs allows us to unravel the intricate techniques employed by the model.

Examining GPT-4's response length and distribution is another crucial aspect of understanding its chat output structure. The model has been designed to generate responses of varying lengths, often mirroring the input message's complexity and depth. By examining patterns in response length, we can better understand the model's tendencies and make informed judgments about its performance.

It is important to note that although GPT-4 is remarkably advanced, it is not exempt from limitations. Analyzing its output structure can help highlight certain shortcomings, such as potential biases, occasional lack of clarity, or an overuse of certain phrases. Understanding these weaknesses empowers us to critically evaluate its output and make thoughtful improvements to the model in future iterations.

To analyze the structure of GPT-4 chat outputs effectively, various techniques can be employed. These include analyzing response lengths, examining the coherence and logical flow of responses, and detecting potential instances of repetition or lack of context. Furthermore, stylistic analysis can help identify patterns and understand how the model generates diverse conversational styles.

Analyzing the structure of GPT-4 chat outputs provides invaluable insights into the inner workings of this advanced conversational AI model. By comprehending the contextual understanding, sentence structuring, coherence, response length, and distribution patterns, we can better appreciate the model's capabilities and identify areas for improvement. Join me in examining the intricate techniques and mechanisms employed by GPT-4 as we embark on this fascinating journey of understanding and analyzing its chat output structure.

5.2 Evaluating Response Coherence and Consistency

When it comes to conversational agents, response coherence and consistency are key factors that determine the success of the interaction. In this context, coherence refers to the logical flow and relevance of the chatbot's responses, while consistency refers to the ability of the chatbot to provide the same information or response for the same user input across different interaction instances. Evaluating these aspects is crucial to develop chatbots that deliver satisfying conversational experiences.

Understanding Coherence:

Coherence in conversational AI refers to the coherent flow of information and ideas within a conversation. It ensures that the chatbot's responses accurately address the user's queries or statements. Incoherent responses can confuse users and hinder the effectiveness of the chatbot. Evaluating coherence involves assessing factors such as the chatbot's ability to understand user intent, its contextual awareness, and its proficiency in generating relevant and coherent responses.

To evaluate response coherence, several techniques are employed, including analyzing conversational context, assessing knowledge retrieval and incorporation, and measuring the overall narrative and topical consistency in the chatbot's responses. These techniques enable developers to identify gaps in the chatbot's understanding and improve its coherence by refining its training data, algorithms, and language models.

Ensuring Consistency:
Consistency is another vital aspect in building reliable and trustworthy conversational agents. It ensures that the chatbot provides consistent responses for similar inputs, regardless of the interaction instance. Inconsistencies can lead to user frustration and loss of trust in the chatbot's capabilities. Evaluating consistency involves examining the chatbot's response patterns across different contexts, user inputs, and system states.

To evaluate response consistency, developers employ various methodologies such as automated testing, user feedback analysis, and comparison with manually curated benchmark datasets. These techniques aim to identify instances where the chatbot provides contradictory or incongruent responses and help improve its training data, algorithms, and dialogue management techniques.

The Role of Evaluation Metrics:
Evaluating response coherence and consistency requires the use of appropriate evaluation metrics. Metrics like perplexity, BLEU scores, and semantic similarity measures are commonly used to determine the accuracy and relevance of the chatbot's responses. These metrics provide quantitative measurements that assist in comparing different chatbot models, identifying areas of improvement, and tracking progress over time.

Moreover, evaluation metrics also help in benchmarking the performance of chatbots against human conversations. By comparing the chatbot's responses with human-generated references or expert annotations, developers can gain insights into the areas where the chatbot excels or falls short, guiding further enhancements in their conversational AI systems.

Evaluating response coherence and consistency plays a crucial role in the development and refinement of conversational AI systems. By ensuring coherent and consistent interactions, chatbots can provide more reliable, accurate, and engaging conversations with users. This evaluation process involves analyzing coherence, refining training data, algorithms, and language models, as well as assessing consistency to rectify any discrepancies or incongruences. When armed with effective evaluation techniques and metrics, developers can pave the way for highly efficient and immersive conversational agents that add significant value to various applications and domains.

5.3 Optimizing for Desired Response Length

We explored various techniques for training and fine-tuning AI chatbots to generate high-quality responses. However, in real-world scenarios, it is often crucial to ensure that the generated responses are of a particular length. For instance, in customer service chatbots, it is essential to provide concise and informative answers, while in conversational chatbots, responses should mimic natural human dialogue.

The optimization techniques necessary for achieving the desired response length in AI chatbots. We discuss the challenges associated with response-length control and explore techniques that can be employed to overcome them.

Understanding the Challenges:
Controlling the response length of AI chatbots presents several challenges. These include:

a. Contextual Awareness: AI chatbots need to be aware of the conversations taking place to generate meaningful responses. However, ensuring the desired response length while preserving context is a challenge, as it requires maintaining the coherence of the conversation.

b. Ambiguity Resolution: Some conversations may involve ambiguous or open-ended discussions. In such cases, it becomes challenging to determine the appropriate length of the response while avoiding abrupt endings or overly verbose replies.

c. Content Relevance: Striking a balance between offering concise yet informative responses can be daunting. Chatbot responses should convey the necessary information without unnecessary verbosity or omitting important details.

Techniques for Optimizing Response Length: To optimize response length in AI chatbots, several techniques can be employed:

a. Length Control Strategies: These strategies involve defining explicit constraints on the response length, such as setting a maximum character or word limit. Ensuring these constraints requires adjusting the model's decoding process to stop generating tokens when the desired length is reached.

b. Conditional Generation: By incorporating user instructions, developers can guide the chatbot to generate responses with desired length characteristics. For example, allowing the user to request a concise or verbose response can help cater to their preferences.

c. Reinforcement Learning: Utilizing reinforcement learning techniques enables the chatbot to learn from feedback and iteratively improve its response generation. By incorporating reward mechanisms that penalize or reward responses based on their length, the chatbot can gradually optimize its replies.

d. Pre-processing Techniques: Adjusting the input conversation or context through pre-processing can help guide the chatbot in generating responses of a specific length. Techniques such as truncating or summarizing the context can be employed to ensure the desired response characteristics.

e. Temperature Sampling: Adjusting the temperature parameter during generation can influence the randomness of the responses. Higher temperatures encourage more exploratory responses that might lead to longer outputs, while lower temperatures yield more deterministic and focused replies.

Evaluating Response Length Optimization:
Determining and evaluating the appropriateness of the response length optimization techniques mentioned above can be achieved through various means:

a. Human Evaluation: Conducting qualitative assessments by involving human evaluators who rate the generated responses based on predefined criteria. This allows for the assessment of the length appropriateness.

b. Automated Metrics: Employing automated metrics, such as BLEU and ROUGE, to measure the quality of generated responses, including length characteristics. These metrics provide a quantitative evaluation of response length optimization techniques.

c. Interactivity: Continuous deployment and iterations with real users can help gauge the effectiveness of response length optimization techniques. Feedback gathered from user interactions assists in improving the overall performance and user satisfaction.

Optimizing the desired response length in AI chatbots is a crucial aspect that determines the quality and usability of chatbot applications across various domains. Employing appropriate strategies and techniques, such as length control, conditional generation, reinforcement learning, pre-processing, and temperature sampling, helps overcome challenges and ensures the generation of responses with the desired length characteristics. Evaluating these techniques through human evaluation, automated metrics, and real-time user interactions leads to continuous improvement and enhances the chatbot's overall performance.

5.4 Transforming Model Outputs into User-Friendly Text

Artificial Intelligence (AI) has revolutionized various industries, ranging from finance to healthcare to transportation, and it is poised to transform the world as we know it. Many newcomers to the field of AI feel overwhelmed by the complex algorithms, mathematical concepts, and technical jargon frequently associated with it. This book is specifically designed to cater to beginners, providing a comprehensive guide to understand and utilize AI techniques and principles.

We will cover various aspects of AI, including its history, major theories and concepts, different learning algorithms, and practical applications. By using precise and accessible language, the book aims to demystify the technicalities surrounding AI, ensuring that readers with little-to-no background in the field can grasp the fundamental ideas behind this revolutionary technology.

By blending theory with practical examples and real-world scenarios, this book presents AI in a tangible and pragmatic manner. Furthermore, we focus on incorporating ethical considerations, as it is essential for AI experts to understand the potential social impact these technologies may have in fostering a better and more equitable world.

Transforming Model Outputs into User-Friendly Text

In the world of Artificial Intelligence, practitioners devote much of their time to building and training models that can generate meaningful and accurate outputs. These outputs typically come in the form of numerical or statistical data that may not be readily understandable to non-experts. However, it is crucial to present and communicate these outputs in a manner that makes them user-friendly and comprehendible to a wider audience.

It focuses on the crucial task of converting these complex and technical results into language that can be easily understood by users. Understanding how to effectively transform the outputs is key in practical applications where these outputs are used to inform decision-making or communicate information to stakeholders.

This chapter starts by discussing the importance of delivering comprehensible and accessible information to end-users, emphasizing the significant impact it has on AI's success. It delves into techniques and strategies that enable transforming AI model outputs seamlessly into user-friendly text, bridging the gap between the language of machines and humans.

The chapter explores various approaches for generating user-friendly text, including summarization techniques that condense lengthy technical outputs into concise and informative summaries. It also investigates natural language processing, a subfield of AI that enables machines to understand and derive meaning from human language, to aid in the successful transformation of output data.

Furthermore, this chapter provides practical guidelines and examples, highlighting best practices for model-output-to-text conversion. It discusses the importance of incorporating domain knowledge and using decision trees to effectively communicate specific AI outputs to different user groups. Moreover, it emphasizes the significance of formatting text, adopting established conventions that users are familiar with to facilitate understanding.

By delving into these concepts, this chapter equips beginners with the necessary knowledge and skills to effectively present AI-generated outputs to diverse audiences. Having a clear and concise understanding of how to transform complex AI outputs into user-friendly text is critical to establishing trust, engagement, and meaningful interactions between human users and AI technologies.

The aim of this chapter, then, is to provide readers with practical insights, grounded in sound theoretical concepts, on transforming model outputs into user-friendly text—a skill that is invaluable in real-world AI applications. Through examples, guidelines, and real-life scenarios, the chapter encourages readers to explore creative ways to make AI outputs accessible, fostering effective communication and understanding between humans and machines.

6. Expanding GPT-4 Chat Knowledge and Capabilities

6.1 Fine-Tuning GPT-4 Chat for Custom Domains

In the vast landscape of Artificial Intelligence, GPT-4 (Generative Pre-trained Transformer 4) stands out as one of the most powerful and advanced language models. It exhibits unparalleled capabilities in generating human-like text, understanding context, and engaging in complex conversations. Although it excels at general knowledge, sometimes we need it to excel even further - to rise above the boundaries of universal information.

So how do we empower GPT-4 to navigate the intricacies and nuances of specific domains? This is precisely where fine-tuning becomes imperative. In this chapter, we delve deep into the process of fine-tuning GPT-4 Chat for custom domains, enabling us to naturally engage with the model on topics aligned with our unique objectives.

Understanding Custom Domains for GPT-4:
Before embarking on the process of fine-tuning, it is pivotal to grasp the concept of custom domains in the context of GPT-4 Chat. A custom

domain pertains to a specific area of knowledge or specialization for which we seek enhanced conversational abilities from the model. For instance, imagine a medical application that necessitates accurate and domain-specific responses about various health conditions. Here, the custom domain would encompass medical knowledge.

Fine-Tuning Principles:
Fine-tuning GPT-4 Chat for custom domains begins by leveraging its pre-trained and generalized understanding. However, during this process, we expose GPT-4 to custom datasets that are exclusively centered around the desired domain to acquire domain-specific masterhood. This enhances the model's performance, making it more accurate, relevant, and personalized.

Dataset Acquisition and Selection:
To effectively fine-tune GPT-4 Chat, we must gather an appropriate dataset tailored to our particular domain. The selection of relevant data plays a crucial role in shaping the capabilities of the finetuned model. A well-crafted dataset ingrains domain-specific knowledge within the model, enabling it to converse intelligently about specialized topics. We navigate through

strategies to find domain-specific data, elucidating its higher yield.

Preparing the Dataset:
Once we have assembled our dataset, preparing it for the fine-tuning process becomes necessary. Noise reduction efforts and structuring the data into trainable format contribute significantly to improved fine-tuning outcomes. We delve into implementation details and best practices of data preparation to maximize its efficiency.

Fine-Tuning Procedure:
The chapter follows a step-by-step elucidation of the process one must undertake to fine-tune GPT-4 Chat successfully. Starting with initiative module modifications, gradual finetuning phases, and ultimately rewarding good output practices, this contextual walkthrough accommodates even beginners in implementing fine-tuning for custom domains.

Evaluating Performance:
A thoroughly fine-tuned GPT-4 model deserves meticulous evaluation to assess its strengths, areas of improvement, and potential issues surrounding adversarial examples. We outline robust evaluation strategies and elaborate on

evaluation metric selections to uphold quality measures.

Scalability and Pitfalls:
With heightened performance in a custom domain, we consider aspects of scalability. Is the model flexible enough for potential updates and expanding specialized knowledge? Additionally, guarding against pitfalls such as overoptimization and biased responses becomes critical when working with fine-tuned models. Understanding these challenges is essential for sustainable usage.

Fine-tuning GPT-4 Chat for custom domains empowers developers, researchers, and builders to tap into the vast capabilities of GPT-4 and achieve tailored experiences. By following the comprehensive guidelines outlined in this chapter, we equip ourselves with the expertise neces+ssary to enhance conversational abilities for various domains. Embrace the transformative potential of fine-tuning to unlock new frontiers in natural language processing and pave the way for more engaging AI applications tailored to specific needs.

6.2 Incorporating External Knowledge Databases

In the fast-paced and technology-driven world we live in today, artificial intelligence has emerged as a transformative force across various industries. As AI continues to evolve and become an integral part of our daily lives, it is crucial for beginners to equip themselves with a comprehensive understanding of the fundamental concepts and techniques in this field. This book serves as the ultimate guide for those looking to delve into the world of AI and lays down the foundation for both theoretical knowledge and practical application.

Artificial intelligence, in its essence, revolves around the concept of creating machines that can mimic human intelligence and perform tasks requiring cognitive abilities like problem-solving, decision-making, and data analysis. One critical aspect of AI research involves incorporating external knowledge databases into intelligent systems to enhance their overall capabilities.

In this chapter, we will explore the significance of incorporating external knowledge databases and their implications for AI applications. External knowledge databases refer to vast repositories of information and structured data that have been collected and organized for various purposes. These databases can include resources such as online encyclopedias, scientific literature databases, or even industry-specific repositories. By leveraging such repositories, AI systems gain access to a vast amount of valuable information, allowing them to make more informed decisions and improve their overall performance.

One of the primary motivations for incorporating external knowledge databases is to mitigate the knowledge gap that exists between human experts and AI systems. While AI has made significant strides in pattern recognition and data analysis, it often lacks the depth and breadth of knowledge possessed by domain experts. By integrating external knowledge databases, we enable AI systems to tap into the collective knowledge of human experts, empowering them to make informed decisions and solve complex problems.

Furthermore, external knowledge databases help AI systems stay up-to-date with rapidly evolving information. In today's dynamic world, new discoveries and advancements occur at a breakneck pace. To keep pace with these changes, AI systems need access to the most recent and relevant information. External knowledge databases serve as a valuable resource for AI systems to continually update their knowledge base, ensuring that they remain robust and effective in their decision-making processes.

Incorporating external knowledge databases also opens up new avenues for AI systems to tackle complex problems. By combining domain-specific information with machine learning algorithms, AI systems can analyze and interpret data in a contextually relevant manner. This integration enables the systems to extract meaningful insights from vast amounts of unstructured data, thereby enhancing their problem-solving capabilities in diverse domains.

However, integrating external knowledge databases into AI systems comes with its own set of challenges. One of the prominent challenges is ensuring the accuracy and quality of the information retrieved from these databases. Since these databases are often obtained from various sources, they may contain errors, biases, or outdated information. An AI system must be equipped with robust mechanisms to validate and verify the accuracy and currency of the retrieved information to avoid potential pitfalls and erroneous conclusions.

Another challenge lies in the complexity of integrating diverse knowledge structures. Knowledge databases vary in their structure and organization depending on the domain and purpose they serve. Aligning and reconciling these structures to extract coherent and meaningful information requires careful consideration and engineering. AI researchers and practitioners need to develop innovative methods and techniques to effectively integrate and harmonize these external knowledge databases, ensuring seamless knowledge utilization.

Incorporating external knowledge databases is a crucial aspect of AI research that enriches the cognitive abilities of intelligent systems. By utilizing these databases, AI systems can bridge the knowledge gap, stay up-to-date with the latest information, and tackle complex problems more effectively. However, integrating external knowledge databases requires addressing challenges related to accuracy, quality, and structural compatibility. As AI continues to advance, researchers and practitioners must explore innovative strategies to leverage these invaluable resources and unlock the full potential of intelligent systems.

6.3 Enhancing GPT-4 Chat's Specific Skills
Fine-tuning GPT-4 Chat
You have learned about the pre-training phase of GPT-4 Chat, which allows it to acquire knowledge from vast amounts of text data. However, as impressive as it may be, GPT-4 Chat cannot provide specialized information without some fine-tuning. In this chapter, we will explore various techniques and methodologies to enhance GPT-4 Chat's capabilities, focusing on its specific skills.

Enhancing GPT-4 Chat's Specific Skills
GPT-4 Chat possesses a wide range of general skills, but it may not be proficient in handling particular tasks or domains. To overcome this limitation, we can employ a variety of techniques to enhance its specific skills.

Domain-Specific Fine-Tuning
To bolster GPT-4 Chat's abilities within a specific domain, we can provide it with targeted training data related to that domain. For instance, if we want GPT-4 Chat to excel in providing medical advice, we can fine-tune it with medical literature, guidelines, and case studies. By fine-tuning within

this specialized domain, GPT-4 Chat will be better equipped to answer medical queries accurately and provide more reliable advice.

Task-Oriented Fine-Tuning

In addition to domain-specific training, we can improve GPT-4 Chat's performance in handling specific tasks. Task-oriented fine-tuning involves training GPT-4 Chat with annotated data specific to that task. For example, if we want GPT-4 Chat to schedule appointments, we can fine-tune it with conversational data that includes examples of appointment scheduling. This approach enables GPT-4 Chat to understand the nuances of the task and generate contextually appropriate responses.

Contextual Reinforcement Learning

GPT-4 Chat can also benefit from contextual reinforcement learning, where it continually learns from real-time interactions with users. By collecting user feedback and utilizing reinforcement learning algorithms, we can train GPT-4 Chat to improve its responses over time. This process allows GPT-4 Chat to adapt and refine its skills based on the specific needs and preferences of its users, leading to more personalized and effective interactions.

Evaluation and Improvement

It is essential to evaluate the performance of GPT-4 Chat after enhancing its specific skills. Robust evaluation metrics can be employed to assess its effectiveness in different domains and specific tasks. Based on the evaluation results, we can identify areas for improvement and implement further enhancements. Continuous evaluation and improvement are crucial to ensuring that GPT-4 Chat remains a reliable and capable conversational AI system.

Ethical Considerations

As we embark on the journey of enhancing GPT-4 Chat's specific skills, it is vital to address the ethical implications of AI advancements. We must consider how GPT-4 Chat's responses may impact individuals, privacy concerns, and potential biases. Responsible AI development involves embedding ethical guidelines and safeguards to mitigate these risks. This chapter will also explore the ethical considerations concerning GPT-4 Chat's specific skill enhancement and provide insights on best practices.

We have discussed various techniques and methodologies to enhance GPT-4 Chat's specific skills. Through domain-specific fine-tuning, task-oriented fine-tuning, and contextual reinforcement learning, we can equip GPT-4 Chat with expertise in specialized domains and tasks. Furthermore, we highlighted the importance of evaluation, continuous improvement, and ethical considerations in the development and deployment of GPT-4 Chat. By employing these strategies, we can unlock the full potential of GPT-4 Chat, creating a more capable and reliable conversational AI system.

6.4 Managing and Training Custom Datasets

As we delve further into the exciting world of artificial intelligence, we must recognize the crucial role that datasets play in shaping the accuracy and performance of our models. Machine learning algorithms heavily rely on data, making it essential to curate and manage datasets strategically. In this chapter, we will explore the intricacies of managing and training custom datasets, equipping beginners like you with the fundamental knowledge needed to navigate this critical aspect of AI research.

In the pursuit of building powerful machine learning models, it is often necessary to create custom datasets specific to your unique problem or application. These datasets act as the foundation upon which your models learn, generalize, and make predictions. By constructing your own datasets, you gain control over the quality, diversity, and relevance of the data, thus tailoring it to optimize model performance.

The process of managing and training custom datasets encompasses several key steps that require careful attention and consideration. We will cover these steps in detail, ensuring that you understand the underlying principles and can effectively apply them to your own AI projects.

To begin, we will explore the process of data collection. This involves gathering relevant data from various sources, such as public databases, web scraping, or even manual data entry. We will discuss techniques for identifying and acquiring suitable data, as well as considerations for maintaining data privacy and legal compliance.

Once the data is collected, we transition to the data preprocessing stage. Raw data is rarely in a format that can be directly fed into machine learning algorithms, so we must apply preprocessing techniques to clean, transform, and enhance the dataset. This may include tasks like removing noise, handling missing values, normalizing or scaling features, and balancing class distributions. We will delve into the intricacies of these preprocessing steps, equipping you with the necessary skills to prepare your dataset for optimal learning.

Next, we move on to data annotation, a critical step in training custom datasets. Annotation involves labeling the collected data with relevant target values or annotations that enable supervised learning. Techniques such as manual annotation, crowdsourcing, or semi-automatic annotation using pretrained models will be explored, along with considerations for quality control and inter-annotator agreement.

Once the dataset is appropriately labeled, we shift our focus to data splitting. A well-divided dataset comprises training, validation, and test sets, each serving a distinct purpose in training and evaluating the model. We will discuss strategies for partitioning the dataset, ensuring an unbiased representation across the different sets, while considering factors such as class imbalances and temporal consistency.

With the foundational steps complete, we can delve into the actual training of machine learning models using custom datasets. We will explore various algorithms and techniques, from traditional approaches like decision trees and support vector machines, to more sophisticated deep learning architectures such as convolutional neural networks (CNNs) and recurrent neural networks (RNNs). Training considerations, including hyperparameter tuning and model evaluation, will be discussed to help you optimize model performance.

Throughout the chapter, we emphasize best practices for managing and training custom datasets. We highlight the importance of data curation, including the need for proper versioning, documentation, and backup strategies. Moreover, we delve into data augmentation techniques, which allow you to increase the size and diversity of your dataset, enhancing model robustness and generalization capabilities.

You will possess a comprehensive understanding of how to manage and train custom datasets, equipping you with the skills to tackle diverse AI challenges. The ability to curate and utilize high-quality datasets will truly empower you as an AI researcher, enabling you to build accurate and effective machine learning models that produce meaningful insights and drive innovation in this rapidly evolving field.

Part III: Best Practices for Effective Conversational AI

7. Designing Engaging and User-Centric Conversations

7.1 Developing Conversation Flows and Structures

In today's fast-paced digital world, conversations with computer systems are becoming increasingly common. From virtual personal assistants to chatbots, interactive voice response systems to customer service bots, and even social humanoid robots, the ability to engage in natural and meaningful conversations with machines has become a sought-after capability.

However, crafting effective conversation flows and structures is no easy task. It requires a deep understanding of language, user intentions, dialogue management, and system capabilities. In this chapter, we delve into the intricacies of developing conversation flows and structures, equipping beginners with valuable insights and techniques to create engaging and dynamic conversations.

To embark on your journey of developing conversation flows, it is crucial to grasp the fundamental concept of dialogues. Dialogues, in the context of AI, refer to the natural back-and-forth exchanges between a user and a machine. Understanding user inputs, generating appropriate responses, and managing the overall flow of the conversation are key components of dialogues.

One significant aspect of conversation development is intent recognition. Intent recognition involves identifying the intention behind a user's input, enabling the system to comprehend and respond accordingly. We explore the various approaches to intent recognition, which include rule-based methods, statistical models, and machine learning techniques.

Another critical factor in conversation flows is context management. Human conversations are heavily influenced by the context in which they occur, and replicating this aspect in machine conversations is essential for an authentic user experience. We delve into context management techniques, such as maintaining conversational history, tracking user states, and leveraging memory models to enhance contextual understanding.

Creating suitable responses is another crucial aspect of conversation development. We delve into the different techniques for response generation, including rule-based templates, data-driven approaches such as retrieval-based methods and generative models, and reinforcement learning-based methods. We also explore the use of natural language understanding (NLU) and natural language generation (NLG) techniques to improve response quality and coherence.

In addition to focusing on individual turns in a conversation, structuring the overall conversation flow is vital to ensure a seamless user experience. We examine dialogue state tracking and management techniques that enable a system to keep track of the progress and dynamics of a conversation. Hierarchical organization, slot-filling structures, and finite-state machines are some of the strategies we cover to structure conversation flows effectively.

Furthermore, we explore the challenges of evaluating and testing conversation systems. Developing metrics to measure the quality of conversations, conducting user studies, and utilizing simulated users are some of the techniques we discuss to assess the performance of conversation flows and structures.

Throughout this chapter, we provide clear examples and practical insights to aid beginners in grasping the intricacies of conversation flow development. From understanding user intents to crafting coherent responses and managing conversation structures, we aim to equip readers with the knowledge and skills necessary to create engaging and effective conversations with machines.

Remember, effective conversation flows and structures are not solely about providing correct answers but also about creating engaging and human-like interactions. So, let us delve into the fascinating world of conversation development and uncover the secrets to building intelligent dialogue systems that captivate users and provide seamless conversational experiences.

7.2 Handling Multiple Turns and Context Transitions

One of the fundamental goals of building conversational agents is to enable natural and engaging interactions between humans and machines. To achieve this, it is essential to develop models that can effectively handle multiple conversational turns and maintain contextual coherence throughout the dialogue.

When humans engage in conversation, they often refer to previous statements and build upon the existing context. Similarly, to create compelling conversational AI systems, it is crucial to capture and utilize preceding dialogue turns and context transitions. By understanding the history of the conversation, AI models can generate appropriate responses, anticipate user intents, and maintain consistency, making the interactions more natural and meaningful.

Handling multiple turns involves managing a sequence of interactions that occur between different participants during a conversation.

These turns may include user inputs, system responses, and follow-up questions. To comprehensively address this challenge, we need to explore techniques that allow AI models to retain and process relevant information from earlier turns, enabling them to generate coherent and contextually appropriate responses.

Context transitions pose another significant obstacle in building conversational AI systems. Transitioning from one conversational context to another is often complex and requires a deep understanding of the dialogue history. For example, when discussing different topics in a conversation, the system needs to remember and reference the relevant information from previous turns to provide accurate and coherent responses. Moreover, context transitions can occur due to changes in user intents, topic shifts, or even interruptions and distractions during the conversation. An effective conversational AI system should seamlessly adapt to such transitions and ensure a smooth continuation of the dialogue.

To address these challenges, researchers have proposed various methods and techniques for handling multiple turns and context transitions in conversational AI systems. These range from traditional rule-based approaches to more advanced machine learning models. Rule-based approaches involve defining explicit rules and patterns to govern the flow of conversation and decision-making. While these methods have been effective in certain domains and limited contexts, they often struggle to handle the complexity and diversity of human conversations.

Machine learning models, on the other hand, leverage vast amounts of training data to learn patterns and generate responses based on the conversation history. These models, such as recurrent neural networks (RNNs) and transformers, have pioneered the field of conversational AI by capturing long-term dependencies and context information. They have demonstrated significant improvements in generating coherent and contextually aware responses. However, challenges still remain, such as handling ambiguous queries, maintaining long-term context, and adapting to abrupt context transitions.

In this chapter, we will explore different approaches and techniques used to handle multiple turns and context transitions in conversational AI systems. We will discuss the advantages and limitations of rule-based approaches and machine learning models. Furthermore, we will delve into recent advancements, such as memory-based models, reinforcement learning, and dialogue state tracking. By understanding these techniques, aspiring AI researchers and practitioners can develop more sophisticated conversational AI systems that are capable of engaging in dynamic and contextually rich dialogues.

Overall, It will provide a comprehensive overview of the key challenges and advancements in handling multiple turns and context transitions in conversational AI systems. By mastering the concepts presented here, readers will gain valuable insights into building robust and natural conversational agents that can adapt to various conversational contexts and provide engaging and meaningful interactions.

7.4 Incorporating Personality and Tone in Conversations

Advancements in artificial intelligence (AI) have revolutionized numerous domains, and one area that has witnessed significant progress is conversational AI. As AI systems become more prevalent in our daily lives, it is crucial for them to develop a distinctive personality and tone to engage users effectively. This chapter delves into the nuances of incorporating personality and tone in conversational AI systems, equipping beginners with the knowledge and tools to create AI systems that are engaging, empathetic, and relatable.

The Importance of Personality and Tone:

When users interact with AI systems, they expect more than just accurate answers; they desire a human-like conversational experience. Incorporating personality and tone into these interactions can greatly enhance the user experience, making it more natural, intuitive, and enjoyable.

Understanding Personality:

Developing a distinct personality for an AI system involves creating a consistent set of characteristics, style, and behavior that align with the system's purpose and target audience. The chosen personality influences the way responses are crafted, ensuring the AI system feels more like a trusted conversational partner than a mere tool.

Factors Influencing Personality:

Several factors influence the personality of an AI system. These include the system's purpose, its intended audience, cultural factors, and the specific domain in which it operates. Additionally, the formality or informality of the language used, the level of humor or seriousness, and the overall demeanor of the AI system all contribute to its personality and tone.

Crafting Tone:

While personality provides the overarching framework, tone allows for flexibility and adaptability within various conversational contexts. Tone refers to the emotional quality or atmosphere conveyed in the conversation, guiding the system's responses in terms of warmth, friendliness, empathy, or professionalism. It is crucial to strike a balance between an adaptable tone and maintaining the system's underlying personality.

Humanizing Conversations:

To ensure AI systems engage users in a human-like manner, it is essential to understand and mimic human conversational behaviors. Incorporating pauses, using natural language, exhibiting empathy, and displaying appropriate emotions are important aspects of building a conversational AI system that feels authentic and relatable.

Ethical Considerations:

While crafting personalities and tones for conversational AI systems, ethical considerations come to the forefront. Developers must be mindful of avoiding biases, stereotypes, or offensive content. Ensuring inclusivity and respecting cultural sensitivities is paramount, as AI systems are used by a diverse range of individuals across the globe.

Balancing Accuracy and Personality:

Adding personality and tone should not come at the expense of accuracy and reliability. It is important to strike a balance between being engaging and providing accurate information. The AI system must prioritize factual correctness while maintaining a conversational flow to keep users actively engaged.

Incorporating personality and tone in conversational AI systems is both an art and a science. This chapter has provided an in-depth exploration of the significance of personality and tone in enhancing user experiences. By understanding the intricacies involved in crafting a system's personality, considering tone, humanizing conversations, and following ethical guidelines, developers can create AI systems that captivate users, making interactions more enjoyable and relatable. With continued advancements in AI research and improvements in natural language processing techniques, conversational AI systems will further evolve to seamlessly blend into our discourse, making interactions with machines feel increasingly human.

8. Addressing Ethical Considerations and Bias
8.1 Ensuring Fairness and Bias Mitigation

As AI technologies become increasingly integrated into various aspects of our daily lives, it becomes crucial to ensure that these systems are fair and unbiased, providing equitable outcomes for all individuals, regardless of their characteristics or backgrounds.

The Need for Fairness:
AI systems have the potential to impact decision-making in critical areas such as employment, finance, law enforcement, healthcare, and many more. However, if these systems are not designed with fairness in mind, they can unintentionally perpetuate or even amplify existing societal biases, leading to discriminatory outcomes and reinforcing inequalities.

Understanding Bias:
Before delving into techniques for bias mitigation, it is essential to grasp the concept of bias as it relates to AI systems. Bias refers to systematic errors or deviations from accuracy in our models or datasets, resulting in unfair and unequal treatment of individuals or groups. These biases can originate from various sources, including data collection processes, algorithm design, or societal prejudices.

Types of Bias:
Bias can manifest itself in different ways within AI systems. One common form is "algorithmic bias," where the predictions or decisions made by an AI

model disproportionately favor or discriminate against certain groups. Another type is "data bias," which occurs when the training data used to create the AI system is unrepresentative, incomplete, or biased itself. Understanding these distinctions is crucial for effectively addressing and mitigating bias in AI systems.

The Impact of Bias:
Biased AI systems can have far-reaching consequences, perpetuating unfairness and discrimination. For instance, biased hiring algorithms might exclude qualified candidates from certain demographic groups. Biased facial recognition systems could incorrectly identify individuals of specific ethnicities, leading to wrongful accusations or increased surveillance of certain communities. Therefore, it is imperative to develop strategies to detect, measure, and mitigate bias in AI systems to ensure equitable outcomes for everyone involved.

Approaches to Fairness and Bias Mitigation:
Thankfully, researchers and practitioners have been working diligently to devise methods to address fairness concerns and mitigate bias in AI systems. This chapter will introduce various approaches, highlighting both pre-processing

techniques that focus on bias detection and mitigation in the data, as well as in-processing and post-processing techniques that aim to mitigate bias within the learning algorithms or after the predictions are made.

Ethical Considerations:
Alongside technical approaches, it is essential to understand the broader ethical considerations associated with fairness and bias mitigation efforts in AI systems. We will delve into issues such as the trade-off between accuracy and fairness, the challenges of defining fairness, and the importance of involving diverse stakeholders in the decision-making process. These considerations are crucial for striving towards ethically responsible AI development.

Empowering AI Developers:
Whether you are an AI practitioner, developer, or simply an interested reader, this chapter aims to equip you with the knowledge and tools necessary to identify, address, and mitigate bias within AI systems. By understanding the intricacies of different bias mitigation techniques and incorporating ethics in AI development, we can collectively foster fairness, inclusivity, and

social progress in the increasingly AI-powered world we inhabit.

Ensuring fairness and mitigating bias in AI systems is of utmost importance as we strive for a future where technology benefits all. By exploring the various approaches to detecting and mitigating bias, understanding the types and impact of bias, and discussing the ethical considerations in this domain, we take a significant step towards creating a more equitable and inclusive AI ecosystem. So let us now delve into the intricacies of fairness and bias mitigation in AI systems, empowering ourselves to contribute to a world that leverages the potential of AI for the betterment of humankind.

8.2 Handling Sensitive and Offensive Content
One of the most intricate challenges is how systems handle sensitive and offensive content, given their potential impact on individuals and society as a whole. Sensitive content encompasses a broad range of material, including but not limited to explicit or violent imagery, hate speech, misinformation, and content that may promote discrimination or harm. Effectively managing this content is essential to

ensure AI systems operate ethically and uphold the values of fairness, diversity, and inclusivity.

The handling of sensitive content requires a multi-faceted approach. Developers and researchers must carefully design and train AI models to recognize these types of content accurately, seeking to mitigate any potential harm caused by their dissemination. However, this process is intricate and delicate due to the subjective nature of offensive material. What one person finds offensive, another may consider acceptable. Therefore, striking the right balance becomes paramount to avoid either over-censorship or under-reaction.

AI models are trained on vast amounts of data, and this plays a pivotal role in their understanding and handling of sensitive content. Data selection and curation become vital steps in ensuring that the training datasets are diverse and adequately represent various perspectives and societal norms. Collaborating with a diverse range of experts, including ethicists, psychologists, sociologists, and representatives from marginalized communities, can help enrich the dataset and enhance the AI system's sensitivity towards avoiding offensive and harmful outputs.

To navigate the complexities of sensitive content, a combination of rule-based approaches and machine learning techniques can be adopted. Rule-based approaches involve setting explicit guidelines and constraints to filter out content that violates ethical norms. These guidelines can be established through collaborations with domain experts, setting thresholds and constraints for what the AI system can produce or recommend. However, rule-based approaches may lack flexibility and can inadvertently restrict access to harmless content or fail to adapt as societal norms evolve.

Machine learning techniques offer an alternative approach, employing algorithms that enable AI systems to learn from patterns in vast datasets. This allows the system to adapt to changing norms over time. However, it is important to ensure these algorithms are regularly updated and evaluated to prevent perpetuating biases or amplifying offensive content. Continuous monitoring and auditing of AI systems are essential to detect and rectify any unintended consequences or biases that may arise.

Another fundamental aspect of handling sensitive and offensive content is providing users with control and agency. Implementing transparent and customizable settings empowers individuals to set their own content preferences and personalize their AI experiences according to their comfort levels. This approach acknowledges that what is sensitive or offensive may vary between individuals, cultures, and regions, thereby ensuring AI systems respect individual boundaries while upholding societal norms.

Addressing and resolving these challenges necessitates a collective effort from various stakeholders involved, including AI researchers, developers, policymakers, and users. Engaging in open dialogue and soliciting feedback from users and impacted communities helps AI systems become more aligned with societal expectations. Ethical considerations surrounding sensitive content should be a collaborative and iterative process, continuously evolving to encompass a wide range of perspectives and fostering inclusivity.

Ultimately, AI systems must be designed and deployed responsibly, taking into account the sensitivity of offensive content to avoid perpetuating harm or further dividing society. By adopting a comprehensive approach that integrates diverse perspectives, rigorous training, constant evaluation, and user empowerment, we can strive to develop AI technologies that respectfully handle sensitive and offensive content, contributing to a more equitable and inclusive future.

8.3 Implementing User Consent and Privacy Measures

As technology advances and we find ourselves increasingly dependent on digital platforms and applications, it is crucial to understand the significance of safeguarding user data and implementing appropriate consent mechanisms.

To begin, we shall discuss the importance of user consent and its relationship to privacy. User consent is the voluntary agreement given by individuals to allow the collection, processing, and storage of their personal data. It forms the cornerstone of ethical data practices and is a legal requirement in many jurisdictions. By obtaining user consent, organizations can establish a transparent and trusted relationship with their users, fostering a sense of control and respect.

We will then explore the various types of consent mechanisms, including explicit, implicit, and opt-in/opt-out approaches. Understanding the differences between these consent models will help you choose the most appropriate method for your specific application or platform. We will delve into the complexities involved in obtaining explicit consent and discuss the challenges surrounding consent fatigue, where users are bombarded with consent requests and may become desensitized to their significance.

Next, we will discuss the implementation of technical measures to ensure user privacy and security. We shall explore the principles of Privacy by Design and Data Minimization, two fundamental concepts that emphasize proactive privacy measures and the minimization of data collection to only what is necessary. We will learn about pseudonymization, anonymization, and encryption techniques that can be employed to protect user data, both in transit and at rest.

In addition to technical measures, we will also delve into organizational and legal aspects of privacy protection. We will discuss the role of privacy policies, terms of service, and the need for clear and comprehensible communication to users regarding data collection, processing, and retention practices. We will explore the significance of conducting Privacy Impact Assessments (PIAs) and the implications of relevant legislation such as the General Data Protection Regulation (GDPR) and the California Consumer Privacy Act (CCPA).

Finally, we shall explore emerging trends and research in the field of user consent and privacy. We will discuss the challenges posed by emerging technologies such as artificial intelligence, machine learning, and Internet of Things (IoT), and how privacy measures need to adapt to ensure the protection and control of user data in these evolving contexts.

You will have a solid foundation in understanding the importance of user consent and privacy measures. Armed with this knowledge, you will be able to design and implement effective privacy practices within your organization, instilling trust and confidence among your user base. So, let us delve into the intricacies of user consent and privacy measures, embarking on a journey to protect and respect the data of users in the digital age.

8.4 Ethical Implications of Open-Ended Conversations

Conversational AI systems have come a long way, enabling interactions that closely resemble human conversations. However, the progress we witness in this field also introduces a set of ethical considerations that must be carefully examined.

Ethics and AI:
Artificial intelligence has advanced to a point where it can engage users in open-ended conversations, allowing for the exchange of broad and complex ideas. While this technology offers numerous benefits, it also brings forth several ethical concerns that must be addressed to ensure responsible and safe deployment.

Privacy and Data Security:
As conversational AI interacts with users, it collects and processes vast amounts of personal data. This raises concerns related to privacy and data security. Users often share highly sensitive information while conversing with AI systems, trusting that their data will be handled securely. Therefore, it becomes essential to establish robust data protection mechanisms to safeguard

users' privacy and prevent unauthorized access or misuse of their personal information.

Transparency and Explainability:
Open-ended conversations involve the use of sophisticated algorithms and deep learning models that may be difficult to comprehend for both users and developers. This lack of transparency can lead to a lack of trust in AI systems. As responsible AI practitioners, it is crucial to design conversational AI that is explainable and transparent to both users and developers. This transparency enhances trust, allowing users to understand how their conversations are being processed and ensuring ethical accountability.

Bias and Fairness:
AI models are trained on vast amounts of data, which can inadvertently encode biases present within that data. Open-ended conversations pose an increased risk of perpetuating biases since the AI system engages in free-flowing conversations with users, potentially reinforcing or amplifying any biases it has learned. It is imperative to address these biases and ensure fair and unbiased conversations to maintain inclusivity and avoid discrimination in AI-driven interactions.

User Manipulation and Persuasion:
Conversational AI has the power to manipulate users and persuade them to make decisions they may otherwise not have made. This raises concerns about the ethical boundaries of AI-driven conversations. It is crucial to establish guidelines and ethical frameworks to prevent the misuse of conversational AI for manipulative purposes and protect users from undue influence.

Accountability and Legal Implications:
As open-ended conversations become more prevalent, questions surrounding accountability and legal responsibility arise. Who should be held accountable if an AI system engages in harmful or malicious conversations? What legal frameworks should govern these interactions? These questions necessitate detailed analysis, offering insights into the legal implications and accountability structures required to ensure responsible use of conversational AI.

While open-ended conversations powered by conversational AI systems offer numerous advantages, they also come with a set of ethical implications that must be acknowledged and addressed. In this chapter, we have explored the ethical considerations related to privacy, transparency, bias, manipulations, and legal implications. By being mindful of these concerns, we can contribute to the development of conversational AI systems that are trustworthy, fair, and respectful of user rights and well-being.

9. Evaluating and Iterating Conversational AI Models

9.1 Designing Evaluation Metrics for Model Performance

In today's AI-driven world, the ability to measure and evaluate the performance of machine learning models has become imperative. As AI technology continues to advance at a rapid pace, designing effective evaluation metrics has become a critical aspect of model development. In this chapter, we delve into the fascinating realm of evaluating model performance to empower beginners with the necessary tools and knowledge.

Evaluation metrics serve as a yardstick to quantify the efficiency and effectiveness of machine learning models. They help us gauge how well a model is performing and provide insights into its strengths and weaknesses. By carefully designing evaluation metrics, we not only enhance our understanding of the model's behavior but also gain valuable insights into its potential for real-world applications.

This chapter begins by laying the foundation for evaluating model performance. We explore the importance of selecting appropriate evaluation metrics that align with our specific objectives and data characteristics. We delve into the concept of generalization, which captures a model's ability to perform well on unseen data, and discuss the significance of choosing evaluation metrics that consider this vital aspect.

Next, we dive deep into the various evaluation metrics commonly used in machine learning. We explore the differences between classification, regression, and clustering evaluation metrics, as each category requires a unique set of metrics to accurately assess model performance.

For classification tasks, we unravel the intricacies of evaluation metrics such as accuracy, precision, recall, F1 score, and area under the receiver operating characteristic curve (AUC-ROC). These metrics help evaluate the performance of models when dealing with binary or multi-class classification problems.

In the realm of regression, we explore metrics like mean squared error (MSE), mean absolute error (MAE), root mean squared error (RMSE), and R-squared. Through understanding these metrics, beginners will gain proficiency in evaluating models' performance when working with continuous target variables.

Additionally, we venture into the realm of clustering evaluation metrics. Clustering, an unsupervised learning technique, seeks to group data points into meaningful clusters. To assess the quality of these clusters, we delve into metrics such as silhouette score, Rand index, and adjusted mutual information score.

While discussing evaluation metrics, we also address the importance of validation and test datasets in model assessment. By distinguishing between these two datasets, beginners will obtain a comprehensive understanding of how evaluation metrics can be tailored to different stages of model development.

Furthermore, we explore the nuances of model evaluation in the context of imbalanced datasets, where the distribution of classes is skewed. We discuss the shortcomings of conventional metrics and introduce alternative measures such as precision-recall curve, area under the precision-recall curve (AUC-PR), and Matthews correlation coefficient (MCC), which are better suited for evaluating models in imbalanced scenarios.

Throughout this chapter, we emphasize the significance of selecting the appropriate evaluation metrics to provide accurate insights into model performance. By grasping the underlying concepts and practical implementation of these metrics, beginners will gain the ability to critically analyze and compare different models to make informed decisions.

Armed with the knowledge from this chapter, beginners will be better equipped to make reliable predictions and contribute to the exciting world of AI research.

9.2 Collecting User Feedback for Model Improvement

Once an AI model has been developed, it is essential to continuously refine it by incorporating valuable insights obtained from user feedback. Gathering user feedback serves a dual purpose: it helps evaluate the model's performance and ensures that the system meets user expectations. Additionally, this feedback plays a pivotal role in training the AI model to enhance its accuracy, robustness, and overall efficiency.

User feedback serves as a valuable resource for identifying and rectifying potential biases, shortcomings, and limitations of the model. It acts as a crucial bridge between the creator of the AI system and the end-users, fostering a collaborative relationship where users actively contribute to the model's iterative improvement.

This explores the intricacies of collecting user feedback, presenting the best practices and methodologies employed in the AI domain. It outlines various strategies and channels for acquiring feedback, ensuring that users find it convenient, accessible, and effortless to provide their valuable opinions.

The Importance of User Feedback:
   User feedback is instrumental in AI research as it provides an objective assessment of the system's performance and helps bridge the gap between user expectations and actual user experiences. It allows researchers and developers

to refine and optimize AI models to better cater to user needs and preferences.

Types of User Feedback:
 User feedback can broadly be categorized into solicited and unsolicited feedback. Solicited feedback is actively sought by the researchers through surveys, interviews, or specific requests, while unsolicited feedback is voluntarily provided by the users without any direct prompting.

Gathering Solicited Feedback:
 This section elaborates on methods such as surveys, interviews, and focus groups as effective means of soliciting user feedback. It explores the importance of clear and concise questions when constructing surveys, conducting insightful interviews to obtain qualitative feedback, and leveraging the collective intelligence of focus groups for in-depth discussions.

Leveraging Unprompted Feedback:
 Users often provide valuable feedback voluntarily, unprompted by any specific request. This section discusses the significance of unsolicited feedback and how to harness it effectively. It explores techniques such as sentiment analysis, natural language processing,

and social media monitoring to systematically gather and analyze unsolicited feedback.

Designing User Feedback Loops:
  Establishing a feedback loop between the AI system and its users is crucial for continuous improvement. This section emphasizes the iterative nature of user feedback and illustrates the implementation of feedback loops. It highlights the significance of timely response and engagement with users in ensuring an active and productive feedback loop.

Handling Biases in User Feedback:
  User feedback can be influenced by various biases, including sampling bias, response bias, and confirmation bias. This section provides insights into identifying and mitigating these biases to ensure the received feedback accurately represents the user base and does not skew the evaluation of the AI system.

Evaluating and Incorporating Feedback:
  This section explores diverse techniques for evaluating user feedback and successfully incorporating it into model improvement. It discusses the merits of quantitative analysis, sentiment analysis, and user segmentation for

efficient feedback evaluation. Additionally, it showcases how to prioritize and implement feedback to enhance the AI system's overall performance.

Balancing User Feedback and Ethical Considerations:
   While collecting user feedback is crucial, it is equally important to consider ethical implications and user privacy. This section emphasizes the need for ethical guidelines and policies to ensure responsible handling of user data and emphasizes the importance of informed consent and privacy protection.

By thoroughly examining the process of collecting user feedback for model improvement, this chapter equips beginners with the necessary knowledge and techniques to actively engage with the user community and enhance their AI models. It encourages a user-centered approach that not only emphasizes performance optimization but also promotes transparency, fairness, and ethical considerations in AI research.

9.3 Iterating and Incrementally Enhancing Conversational AI

Conversational AI has witnessed remarkable advancements in recent years, transforming the way we interact with machines. This chapter delves into the crucial concept of iterating and incrementally enhancing Conversational AI systems, paving the way for their continuous improvement and adaptation.

Iterating refers to the process of repeating a set of steps or actions with the aim of refining and perfecting a system over time. When applied to Conversational AI, iterating becomes an invaluable approach for honing the system's abilities and optimizing its performance. By continually revisiting and improving upon the system's existing features, developers and researchers can systematically enhance the overall user experience and achieve higher levels of user satisfaction.

Incremental enhancement plays a pivotal role in the iterative process, facilitating steady and continual progress. Instead of attempting to revolutionize the entire Conversational AI system in a single update, incremental enhancement promotes the idea of making small, incremental improvements that can be easily tested, evaluated, and deployed. This iterative approach allows for the swift identification and resolution of issues, ultimately leading to a smoother and more efficient conversational experience.

One of the key advantages of adopting an iterative and incremental approach is the ability to gather real-time feedback from users. By deploying the enhanced system to a limited audience, developers can collect valuable insights and receive direct input from users, helping them assess the effectiveness of implemented improvements. This user-centric approach enables AI researchers and developers to better understand user preferences, pain points, and evolving expectations, thereby empowering them to guide subsequent iterations towards a more tailored and personalized user experience.

Furthermore, iterative and incremental enhancements facilitate the integration of emerging technologies and research breakthroughs. The Conversational AI field witnesses rapid advancements, with novel techniques, algorithms, and frameworks continually surfacing. By embracing an iterative mindset, developers can evaluate, adapt, and incorporate these advancements into their systems, ensuring that their conversational agents remain at the forefront of AI innovation.

Iterating and incrementally enhancing Conversational AI is a cyclical process, comprising various stages such as planning, developing, testing, and refining. These stages are not necessarily linear, as they often overlap and inform each other. Starting with thorough planning, developers outline the goals and objectives they aim to achieve in each iteration, ensuring a clear direction for enhancement efforts. The development phase involves implementing the planned improvements, leveraging the latest technological advancements and research findings.

Subsequently, rigorous testing and evaluation are crucial to identify the effectiveness and impact of the implemented enhancements. A variety of metrics, both objective and subjective, can be employed to assess the system's performance, including conversational quality, user engagement, task completion rates, and user satisfaction. Based on the evaluation results, developers can refine the system and fine-tune its components, iteratively enhancing its conversational abilities, and addressing any identified shortcomings.

It is important to note that the iterative and incremental approach does not guarantee instant perfection. Rather, it sets the foundation for constant progress and evolution. By embracing this methodology, developers can gradually build upon the system's strengths, address weaknesses, and adapt to the ever-changing needs and expectations of users.

The iterative and incremental enhancement of Conversational AI systems is a vital process that ensures continuous improvement, adaptability, and user-centricity. By iteratively refining and enhancing their conversational agents, developers can create more engaging and effective systems, fostering a seamless interaction between humans and machines. Through real-time feedback, integration of emerging technologies, and rigorous evaluation, Conversational AI can continue to evolve, offering users increasingly satisfying and personalized conversational experiences.

10. Real-world applications and Use Cases
10.1 Customer Support and Chatbots

Customers have high expectations when it comes to obtaining assistance or resolving issues, and businesses must adapt to these evolving needs. This is where chatbots, powered by artificial intelligence (AI), come into play. Chatbots are virtual assistants that can engage with customers, understand their queries, and provide relevant solutions or information in real time. In this chapter, we will explore the fascinating world of customer support through chatbots, discussing their benefits, implementation strategies, and potential challenges.

Understanding Customer Support:

Customer support is the process of assisting customers through various channels, such as phone calls, emails, or live chats, to address their concerns, provide information, and resolve issues they might encounter. Traditional customer support methods involve direct interaction between customers and human agents. However, this approach has limitations, including scalability, human error, and the potential for inconsistent responses.

The Rise of Chatbots:

To address these challenges, organizations are embracing chatbots as a powerful tool in their customer support arsenal. Chatbots can provide instant and accurate responses to customer queries, ensuring a consistent and efficient support experience. These AI-powered virtual agents are available 24/7, eliminating the need to wait for human assistance or adhere to limited support hours.

Benefits of Chatbots in Customer Support:

Instantaneous Assistance: Chatbots can provide immediate responses to customer queries, significantly reducing waiting times and improving customer satisfaction.

Scalability: Unlike human agents, chatbots can handle multiple customer interactions simultaneously, ensuring prompt support even during high-volume periods.

Consistency: Chatbots offer consistent responses and information, reducing the chances of human error or conflicting information that may arise from different human agents.

Cost Efficiency: Implementing chatbots for customer support can be more cost-effective over time, as they require fewer resources and are capable of handling a substantial volume of inquiries.

Personalization: Advanced chatbots can be designed to understand customer preferences and tailor their responses accordingly, creating a more personalized support experience.

Implementing Chatbots in Customer Support:

Integrating chatbots into customer support requires careful planning and execution. Here are some key steps to consider:

Identify Use Cases: Determine the specific areas of customer support that can benefit from deploying chatbots. Whether it's frequently asked questions, order tracking, or basic troubleshooting, identifying use cases helps in aligning chatbots with customer needs.

Design Conversational Flows: Develop chatbot conversations that resonate with your customers. By mapping out potential dialogues, you can ensure a smooth and effective interaction that meets customer expectations.

Utilize Natural Language Processing (NLP): NLP enables chatbots to understand and process human language effectively. By leveraging NLP techniques, your chatbot can accurately interpret and respond to customer queries.

Test and Refine: Iterative testing is crucial to ensure chatbots are delivering accurate and helpful responses. Continually refine your chatbot's performance by analyzing customer feedback and making necessary adjustments.

Challenges and Considerations:

While chatbots bring numerous benefits to customer support, there are additional considerations to keep in mind:

Complexity of Queries: Chatbots may struggle to handle complex or ambiguous queries, requiring human intervention or fallback options to ensure customer satisfaction.

Emotional Intelligence: Chatbots lack emotional intelligence, which can be essential when dealing with frustrated or upset customers. Organizations should have contingency plans in place to transfer interactions to human agents when required.

Language Limitations: Chatbots may face challenges in understanding variations in language, slang, or colloquial expressions. Training the chatbot on different linguistic patterns is crucial for accurate comprehension.

10.2 Virtual Assistants and Personalized Interactions

The emergence of artificial intelligence has revolutionized the way we interact with technology. Virtual assistants have become an integral part of our lives, seamlessly integrating into our daily routines. From smartphones to smart speakers, virtual assistants provide us with personalized interactions, assisting us in various tasks such as answering questions, managing schedules, and even controlling smart home devices.

In this chapter, we delve deep into the world of virtual assistants, unraveling their capabilities, functionalities, and the underlying technologies that power their intelligence. We explore the intricate details of how these assistants adapt to our needs, offer personalized experiences, and cater to our individual preferences.

Virtual assistants, often powered by machine learning and natural language processing algorithms, are designed to understand and interpret human commands and queries. These sophisticated technologies enable assistants to listen to spoken language, process it, and provide contextually accurate responses. By employing advanced language models, virtual assistants can decipher the intent behind a question, analyze the context, and retrieve relevant information or perform tasks with proficiency.

But what truly sets virtual assistants apart is their ability to personalize interactions. By learning from our interactions, preferences, and historical data, these assistants can tailor their responses and recommendations to cater to our individual needs. They become familiar with our routines, adapt to our speech patterns, and even predict our preferences based on behavioral patterns.

The technology behind personalization in virtual assistants relies heavily on machine learning techniques such as deep learning and reinforcement learning. These algorithms allow virtual assistants to continually improve their understanding of user preferences, adapt to changes, and deliver more accurate and relevant responses as time progresses.

Virtual assistants offer a wide range of functionalities, including information retrieval, task management, and entertainment. They serve as reliable sources of information, retrieving data from vast knowledge bases and presenting it in a concise and understandable format. Whether you need to find the latest news, get weather updates, or gather information on a particular topic, virtual assistants are there to assist you.

In addition to information retrieval, virtual assistants excel at managing tasks and schedules. From setting reminders and alarms to organizing meetings and sending emails, they help us stay on top of our daily responsibilities. With natural language processing capabilities, virtual assistants make these tasks more streamlined and intuitive, simplifying our lives by reducing the effort required for organization and planning.

Moreover, virtual assistants have become our companions, entertaining us and enhancing our leisure activities. They offer personalized music recommendations, suggest movies based on our preferences, and even engage in conversations to keep us entertained. With advancements in emotional intelligence and sentiment analysis, virtual assistants are becoming more adept at understanding our moods and providing appropriate responses or assistance.

As virtual assistants continue to evolve, the challenges and opportunities in this field are immense. Ethical considerations surrounding privacy and data protection arise, demanding transparent and responsible approaches to ensure user trust. Furthermore, research and development efforts are ongoing to enhance the naturalness of interactions, diversify cultural understanding, and foster empathy within virtual assistants.

Virtual assistants have transformed the way we interact with technology, providing us with personalized and intelligent experiences. By leveraging advanced machine learning and natural language processing techniques, these assistants can understand our commands, retrieve information, and perform tasks with remarkable accuracy. Their ability to adapt to our preferences, learn from our interactions, and personalize interactions offers immense convenience and efficiency. As virtual assistants continue to advance, the possibilities for this technology are endless, promising even more seamless and natural interactions in the future.

10.3 Gaming and Interactive Storytelling
Video games have revolutionized the entertainment industry, captivating millions of players worldwide with their immersive and interactive experiences. One of the key elements that make modern games so engaging is the integration of interactive storytelling. In this chapter, we will delve into the fascinating world where gaming and storytelling merge, exploring the techniques, technologies, and the future of gaming narratives.

Gaming and Interactive Storytelling

The Evolution of Storytelling in Gaming:

The earliest video games primarily focused on providing simple gameplay experiences without emphasizing narrative elements. However, as technology advanced, game developers recognized the importance of incorporating compelling stories to enhance users' immersion and emotional attachment. This section takes you on an insightful journey of how storytelling has evolved in gaming, from the text-based adventures of the past to the complex narratives of modern open-world games.

The Power of Interactive Storytelling:

Interactive storytelling enables players to actively participate in the game's narrative, giving them agency and influencing the outcome of the story. This section explores the unique advantages and challenges posed by interactive storytelling, delving into the impact it has on player engagement, emotional investment, and overall gameplay experience.

Narrative Structures in Games:

Creating compelling narratives within video games requires meticulous planning and structure. This section introduces various narrative structures commonly employed in gaming, such as linear narratives, branching narratives, and emergent narratives. We will explore the strengths and limitations of each structure and discover how they shape the player's experience.

Character Development and Player Agency:

Engaging characters play a crucial role in any narrative-driven game. This section discusses how game developers craft multi-dimensional characters who interact seamlessly with the game's environment and respond dynamically to player choices. We will also examine the delicate balance between player agency and maintaining a coherent narrative arc.

Technology and Tools for Interactive Storytelling:

Advancements in technology have expanded the possibilities for interactive storytelling in gaming. This section provides an overview of the tools and technologies used to create captivating narratives, including dialogue systems, choice-based mechanics, and dynamic storytelling techniques. We will explore how these tools empower game developers to create personalized and immersive storytelling experiences.

The Future of Gaming and Interactive Storytelling:

As we peer into the future of gaming, we envision even more ambitious and innovative approaches to interactive storytelling. This final section explores emerging trends, such as virtual reality (VR), augmented reality (AR), and artificial intelligence (AI), and their potential impact on the future of gaming narratives. We will discuss how these technologies can further enhance the immersion, interactivity, and emotional depth of gaming experiences.

Gaming and interactive storytelling have become inseparable, igniting players' imaginations and transporting them into captivating virtual worlds. Through this chapter, we have uncovered the evolution, techniques, and technologies behind interactive storytelling in gaming. By understanding these concepts, you will gain a deeper appreciation for the narratives that unfold within video games, and perhaps even be inspired to create your own compelling gaming experiences in the future. So, let's embark on this exciting journey into the world of gaming and interactive storytelling!

10.4 Educational and Language Learning Tools

Various technological advancements have paved the way for innovative educational tools that aim to enhance learning experiences. As a beginner exploring the realm of educational and language learning tools, it is important to understand their significance, potential benefits, and popular examples. In this section, we will explore the vast array of tools designed to support educational pursuits and facilitate language learning.

Understanding Educational Tools:
Educational tools refer to a variety of software, applications, or devices specifically designed to assist students and educators in their learning journeys. These tools are thoughtfully created to cater to different learning styles, topics, and age groups. They often provide interactive and engaging experiences that enhance comprehension, retention, and overall academic performance.

Benefits of Educational Tools:
Educational tools offer numerous advantages for both learners and educators. Firstly, these tools foster student engagement by presenting information in an interactive and visually appealing format. By incorporating aspects such as gamification and multimedia content,

educational tools create an immersive learning environment that enhances motivation and knowledge acquisition.

Secondly, these tools provide personalized learning experiences. Through adaptive algorithms, educational tools can assess an individual's strengths and weaknesses, tailoring content and exercises to meet their specific needs. This individualized approach to education helps students progress at their own pace, boosting their confidence and ultimately improving their learning outcomes.

Furthermore, educational tools often offer real-time feedback and performance tracking. Students can receive immediate responses to their answers, enabling them to identify areas where improvement is required. Likewise, educators can monitor students' progress and determine the effectiveness of their teaching strategies, allowing for timely intervention and adjustment.

Examples of Educational Tools:
Virtual Reality (VR) and Augmented Reality (AR): These immersive technologies transport learners to virtual worlds where they can explore historical

landmarks, conduct virtual science experiments, or practice foreign language conversations.

Learning Management Systems (LMS): LMS platforms provide a centralized hub for organizing and delivering educational content. They often include features such as online assignments, discussion boards, and grade management tools, facilitating seamless communication and assessment between educators and students.

Interactive Whiteboards: These digital successors to traditional blackboards allow educators to present dynamic content, including images, videos, and interactive exercises. They promote collaboration and active participation, generating a dynamic classroom environment.

Language Learning Tools:
In addition to general educational tools, language learning tools have gained significant popularity due to the growing demand for language acquisition in today's interconnected world. Such tools provide valuable resources for beginners and advanced learners alike, offering personalized language learning experiences that cater to individual goals and proficiency levels.

Benefits of Language Learning Tools:
Language learning tools offer unique opportunities for individuals looking to develop their language skills. Firstly, these tools provide convenient access to language learning materials, eliminating the need for physical textbooks or costly language classes. Users can conveniently access language learning tools via smartphones, tablets, or computers, making it possible to study anytime and anywhere.

Secondly, language learning tools often incorporate interactive exercises and simulations, allowing learners to practice their language skills in a realistic context. These tools offer pronunciation practice, vocabulary building exercises, grammar drills, and even conversation simulations, providing essential practice opportunities without the need for a language partner.

Examples of Language Learning Tools:
Language Learning Applications: There is a wide range of mobile applications available that offer language courses tailored to various proficiency levels. These apps often provide vocabulary and grammar exercises, audio recordings for

pronunciation practice, and even live chat options with native speakers.

Online Language Learning Platforms: Web-based platforms dedicated to language learning offer comprehensive courses that cover all aspects of language acquisition. They often have an extensive library of resources, including videos, interactive exercises, and forums for learner interaction.

Language Exchange Platforms: These platforms connect individuals interested in language exchange, providing an opportunity to practice conversational skills with native speakers. Users can participate in conversations with others learning their target language, fostering mutually beneficial language learning experiences.

Educational and language learning tools have revolutionized the way we acquire knowledge and develop language skills. Their engaging and interactive nature, coupled with the ability to personalize learning experiences, have made them invaluable resources for learners of all ages. By embracing the advantages offered by educational and language learning tools, beginners can enhance their learning journey, paving the way for a more prosperous and successful educational experience.

10.5 Future Possibilities and Industry Adoption

The future of artificial intelligence holds immense possibilities that extend beyond what we have witnessed and accomplished thus far. Advancements at the cutting edge of AI research continue to emerge, propelling its capabilities to new heights. While our current applications range from natural language processing and computer vision to machine learning and robotics, the growth potential of AI is poised to unlock further realms of innovation.

One compelling direction AI is likely to forge ahead with addresses the personalized experiences it can offer. By intricately understanding human behavior and preferences, driven by enormous amounts of data extracted from various sources, AI systems could create tailored experiences across industries. Individuals will find delight in more personalized services ranging from immersive entertainment experiences and highly adaptive education platforms, to healthcare interventions personalized on one's unique genetic makeup and health data.

Continuing along this path, we anticipate the integration of augmented intelligence, which connotes the close collaboration of human intelligence alongside AI. This hybrid approach could revolutionize workplaces across diverse disciplines, opening doors to problem solving at an unrivaled efficiency and scale. Businesses and professionals alike might rely on AI systems as invaluable partners, leveraging its processing power, data analysis capabilities, and efficient decision-making to achieve exceptional outcomes. Likewise, automated services relying on AI intelligence may become immensely sophisticated and ubiquitous, wielding real-time predictive capabilities, guaranteeing convenience like never before.

Furthermore, we envision remarkable advancements in the field of machine ethics, shaping AI deployments in a highly responsible and ethical manner. The debate on moral agency and autonomy within AI systems becomes increasingly relevant as we witness more sophisticated machines, equipped with substantial decision-making capacity. Striking the right balance between the automation and discretion of AI systems will remain key to further explorations in a wide array of fields - such as autonomous vehicles, finance, governance, and health. Careful regulations and industry standards will dictate the integrity to ensure AI endowments are always in alignment with significant ethical considerations.

In terms of industry adoption, we can confidently say that AI technologies are gaining remarkable traction across a multitude of sectors. Having outgrown a shroud of theoretical speculation, AI is taken seriously as a driving force of transformation, fostering efficiency, and delivering tangible value to varied industries. AI innovations offer unparalleled improvements in customer experiences, enhanced quality control, optimal decision-making, streamlined processes, and increased productivity.

In healthcare, AI emerges as a facilitator of improved diagnostics precision, personalized treatment recommendations, and better patient outcomes. By conquering challenges such as accurate medical image analysis, disease prediction, and automating routine administrative tasks, AI significantly transforms the medical landscape, ultimately leading to enhanced discovery and customized interventions.

Additionally, AI's imprint on finance and banking sectors comes in the form of accurate risk assessments, fraud detection, and streamlined customer interactions powered by natural language processing. Embracing AI grants financial practitioners a competitive edge, enabling careful and deep analysis of trends, autonomously adjusting investment portfolios, and improving customer-centric experiences.

Another notable industry-enhancing AI holistically integrates the approach taken in the agricultural domain. Sensors, drones, and deep learning models oversee crop health inspections, irrigation systems analysis, and precise proper resource allocation. Ultimately, smart agriculture promotes sustainable practices, ensuring optimized yield and managing challenges such as pests persuasively.

Through observing such industry advancements, it becomes apparent that successful further adoption of AI critically relies on cultivating a workforce adept at tapping into its vast merits. The proactive education of professionals, regardless of their domain expertise, ideally traverses organizations adopting AI holistically.

Skilling the workforce to use AI as a valued tool not only enhances efficiency and productivity levels but also prepares society to leverage meaningful insights considerately for long-term socio-economic benefit.

As we draw nearer to the impressive manifestations AI technology promises, a world powered by fruitful cooperation between human intellect and machine counterparts feels relentlessly closer. Society at large will undoubtedly grapple with the ethical questions arising due to increased reliance on AI agents. Striking this balance while focusing on beneficial harmonization between humans and AI ensures unstoppable transformative potential while maintaining our agency to realize its substantial utility.

Conclusion and Future Outlook:
11. Recap of Key Concepts and Takeaways
As you have progressed through the chapters, you've familiarized yourself with the exciting world of AI, starting from its definition, history, and applications, to the various techniques and algorithms employed in AI systems. This recap will serve as a comprehensive summary,

highlighting the essential facets of AI that you have explored in your journey so far.

Definition and History of AI:
The opening chapters acquainted you with the definition of AI, which refers to the creation of intelligent machines capable of mimicking human-like behaviors. We discussed the roots of AI, dating back to antiquity, and traced its development through different historical milestones. From the early days of AI research to the present, we have witnessed immense progress, leading us towards the AI-enabled world we live in today.

AI Techniques:
You learned about the different techniques employed in AI, including symbolic AI, machine learning (ML), and deep learning (DL). Symbolic AI utilizes a rule-based approach, while ML relies on algorithms to learn patterns from data. DL, on the other hand, utilizes artificial neural networks to simulate human-like thought processes. Understanding these techniques will help you appreciate the versatility and range of AI applications.

Core AI Concepts:

We explored core concepts such as data, features, labels, and models. Data is the raw input that an AI system uses to learn, while features refer to the meaningful patterns extracted from the data. Labels are the desired outputs or predictions that an AI system aims to achieve, and models are the mathematical representations that capture the relationships between data and labels.

Machine Learning Algorithms:
This section delved into various fundamental machine learning algorithms, including classification, regression, clustering, and reinforcement learning. Classification is used to categorize data into predefined classes, regression predicts continuous values, clustering identifies patterns and groups in data, and reinforcement learning enables an AI agent to learn and make decisions through interactions with its environment.

Deep Learning and Neural Networks:
We further explored deep learning, a subset of ML, by examining neural networks. Neural networks are designed to mimic the functioning of the human brain, consisting of interconnected layers of artificial neurons. You gained an

understanding of feedforward and recurrent
neural networks and the powerful learning
capabilities they possess.

AI Ethics and Implications:
Recognizing the significance of ethical
considerations in AI, we explored the ethical
dilemmas associated with its development and
application. We discussed bias, fairness,
transparency, accountability, and privacy
concerns. Understanding the potential societal
impact of AI will empower you to approach AI
development and deployment responsibly and
ethically.

AI Applications:
Throughout this book, we explored the myriad of
AI applications across diverse domains, including
healthcare, finance, education, transportation, and
entertainment. From disease diagnosis to stock
market predictions and personalized learning, AI
has the potential to revolutionize numerous
industries, making substantial contributions to
society at large.

The Future of AI:
To conclude our journey, we looked into future
prospects and challenges within the field of AI.

As AI continues to evolve, we discussed the potential for augmented intelligence, human-AI collaboration, and the need for ongoing research and development to address emerging challenges and ensure AI's responsible use.

You have gained a solid foundation in AI, exploring its definition, techniques, algorithms, core concepts, ethical considerations, applications, and future prospects. Armed with this knowledge, you are equipped to join the ranks of those driving the future of AI and contribute to shaping a world where intelligent machines coexist harmoniously with humanity.

12. The Future of Conversational AI and GPT

Artificial Intelligence (AI) has rapidly become an integral part of our daily lives, revolutionizing various fields such as healthcare, finance, transportation, and entertainment. AI-powered technologies possess the ability to replicate human intelligence and perform complex tasks efficiently and accurately. The significance of AI in driving innovation and transforming industries cannot be overstated. However, as the journey of AI progresses, researchers and developers continually face a plethora of challenges while also uncovering exciting opportunities.

One of the key challenges faced by AI researchers revolves around the complexity of building intelligent systems. The development of AI models requires teams of researchers proficient in computer science, mathematics, and statistics, collaborating to create algorithms that can comprehend vast amounts of data and derive insightful conclusions. This complexity demands a deep understanding of machine learning methodologies, optimization techniques, and data analysis. Furthermore, innovative research is essential to improve upon existing AI approaches and pave the way for new advancements. Overcoming such complexities and producing relevant research contributes towards the overall progress of AI technology.

Another significant challenge lies in dataset acquisition and processing. AI models rely on large volumes of carefully collected and labeled datasets to learn from. However, acquiring extensive and diversified datasets often presents hurdles due to limited availability, privacy constraints, and the unreliability of some sources. Furthermore, preparing datasets with accurate annotations necessitates meticulous annotation efforts sometimes carried out by huge teams of annotators. AI researchers must address these challenges, ensuring the quality and representativeness of data to avoid biased or skewed model outcomes.

Ethics and accountability form indispensable aspects of AI development, posing themselves as critical challenges to both researchers and developers. As AI technology makes decisions autonomously, issues such as transparency, fairness, and moral decision making come into play. Researchers face the daunting task of creating models with mechanisms to address concerns such as algorithmic biases, privacy violation risks, and unintended discrimination. There is an emerging responsibility to promote inclusivity and affirmative action within the AI design philosophy, potential regulated guidelines.

Technical limitations also comprise another significant challenge for AI researchers and developers. Despite the vast capabilities of AI systems, they are constricted by existing hardware limitations that affect model training speed, energy consumption, and online inference. Bridging this gap between optimal hardware utilization and AI algorithms efficiency plays a crucial role in advancing AI technology. Efforts are ongoing to develop efficient algorithms, simultaneously exploring specialized hardware options like GPUs and neural processing units (NPUs) to enhance AI system performance. Continued optimization efforts are vital in establishing resourceful and practical AI models.

While overcoming a myriad of challenges, AI researchers and developers are greeted with numerous opportunities as technology progresses further. The dynamic, ever-changing landscape of AI offers immense potential for pushing the boundaries of what is possible. Striving for improved problem-solving techniques can fuel innovation in areas such as robotics, healthcare diagnostics, autonomous vehicles, virtual assistants, and customer service automation.

Furthermore, AI technology acts as an enabler for developing advanced systems that can significantly impact our society positively. It has the potential to accelerate scientific research, corrosion analysis, weather modeling, and drug discovery, mitigating major global issues in less time. The collaboration of AI with other ingenious solutions, such as the Internet of Things (IoT) and Big Data, opens avenues to create autonomous smart systems that improve crop yield management, facility management, and predictive maintenance.

AI researchers and developers also stand at the forefront of another opportunity – imparting ethical considerations while fostering AI progress. By taking a proactive stance on developing responsible and accountable AI systems, advocates aim to curtail negative implications and augment trust from users. Innovative approaches that emphasize data privacy protection, ethical frameworks, and interpretability assurance create a fertile environment for future advancements while mitigating potential risks.

AI research and development face intricate challenges, shaping their roadmap towards the continued advancements of machine intelligence. Each hurdle tackled contributes to refining AI capabilities for supporting nearly every aspect of our daily lives and providing novel solutions to grand challenges. Opportunities awaiting AI researchers and developers thrive beyond scientific achievements and extend into shaping a responsible and prosperous society embedded with AI solutions aiding as supplements for human intelligence.

13. Challenges and Opportunities for AI Researchers and Developers

As AI systems become more adept at performing complex tasks and replicating human cognitive abilities, it is crucial for AI researchers and developers to confront the challenges and grasp the numerous opportunities inherent in this domain. This chapter aims to provide a comprehensive understanding of the obstacles faced and the potential benefits awaiting professionals venturing into the exciting realm of AI.

Complex Algorithms and Computations:
AI research and development necessitate the design and implementation of intricate algorithms and computational models. Developing these algorithms requires a deep understanding of machine learning techniques and statistical analysis. The chapter explores various algorithms used in AI, such as neural networks, decision trees, and genetic algorithms, and highlights the expertise required to configure and optimize these models effectively.

Data Availability and Quality:
AI systems heavily rely on vast quantities of data to learn, generalize, and make informed decisions. However, accessing suitable datasets and ensuring data quality pose significant challenges. The chapter delves into the difficulties faced when collecting and curating data, providing insights on strategies for acquiring diverse and representative datasets while addressing concerns related to data privacy, bias, and fairness. It also discusses techniques for data augmentation, synthesis, and annotation to tackle data scarcity issues.

Ethical and Legal Considerations:
As AI systems become more powerful and pervasive, ethical and legal dimensions play a crucial role in shaping responsible AI development. The chapter explores the ethical dilemmas surrounding AI, such as bias in decision-making, privacy infringements, and the potential for automation-induced job displacement. It also addresses regulatory frameworks, like the General Data Protection Regulation (GDPR) and algorithmic transparency requirements, enabling AI researchers and developers to navigate the ethical and legal landscape effectively.

Interpretability and Explainability:
The inherent complexity of AI models often renders them as "black boxes," making it challenging to understand and interpret their decision-making processes. This lack of interpretability raises concerns regarding accountability, fairness, and trustworthiness of AI systems. The chapter investigates different techniques and methodologies aimed at enhancing interpretability and explainability in AI models, allowing researchers and developers to build more transparent and understandable systems.

System Robustness and Security:
Protecting AI systems from adversarial attacks and ensuring their robustness is a critical concern. The chapter discusses the vulnerabilities of AI models to adversarial attacks, where inputs are carefully manipulated to mislead the system's output. It also explores secure machine learning techniques and adversarial training approaches, providing readers with insights into fortifying AI systems against potential threats.

Human-AI Collaboration:

Efficient collaboration between humans and AI systems holds immense potential for solving complex problems. However, designing effective human-AI interfaces and integrating AI seamlessly into human workflows present challenges. This chapter explores human-centered design principles, conversational AI, and other approaches to facilitate natural and productive collaboration between humans and AI systems, creating synergies that amplify capabilities and augment human intelligence.

Continual Learning and Adaptability:
The ability of AI systems to learn from new data and adapt to evolving environments is vital for their long-term success. The chapter investigates lifelong and continual learning techniques, exploring how AI models can efficiently accumulate knowledge, avoid catastrophic forgetting, and adapt to changing circumstances. It also delves into reinforcement learning algorithms that enable AI systems to learn through trial and error, opening new avenues for real-world applications.

Collaboration and Open-Source Initiatives:
Advancing AI research and development requires collaborative efforts and open exchange of

knowledge. The chapter highlights different collaborative models, academic-industry partnerships, and open-source initiatives, emphasizing the value of sharing code, datasets, and research findings. It also delves into the benefits and challenges associated with interdisciplinary collaboration, encouraging aspiring AI researchers and developers to engage with a diverse community of experts.

Acknowledgment
The process of writing a book involves numerous individuals who play invaluable roles in its creation and success. These individuals can range from friends and family who provide encouragement and support, to experts and professionals who offer their knowledge and expertise. In recognition of their contributions, it is customary and gracious to include an acknowledgment section in a book.

Acknowledgment is the act of expressing appreciation and gratitude towards those who have exerted efforts, provided assistance, or contributed to the development of a literary work. It offers authors an opportunity to publicly acknowledge the individuals who have made a meaningful impact throughout the book's journey.

Writing an acknowledgment section serves several purposes. Firstly, it allows authors to recognize the emotional and practical support they have received from their loved ones, including their families, partners, or close friends. These individuals offer encouragement, understanding, and often act as a sounding board during the creative process. Their unwavering support plays a crucial role in an author's ability to bring their book to life.

Furthermore, an acknowledgment section provides a platform for authors to express gratitude to the editorial team and professionals who have played a pivotal role in shaping the book's content and structure. These individuals, such as editors, proofreaders, and literary agents, bring their expertise to enhance the quality and coherence of the final product. Their diligent efforts help refine the author's ideas and ensure the book's readability and accuracy.

In addition to friends, family, and professionals, authors may also wish to acknowledge mentors and advisors who have guided and inspired them throughout their writing journey. These individuals offer valuable insights, support, and guidance, helping authors navigate challenges and refine their craft. Their wisdom and expertise contribute immensely to an author's growth and development as a writer.

Moreover, authors may choose to express gratitude to colleagues, mentors, or experts within their field who have shared their knowledge and experiences. These individuals provide invaluable insights and perspectives that enrich the book's content and credibility. Their contributions contribute to the book's authority and deepen its impact on readers.

Furthermore, authors may choose to thank individuals who have provided access to resources or facilitated research endeavors. These individuals can include librarians, archivists, or professionals who have extended their expertise and made their resources available. Such contributions enable authors to conduct thorough research and provide accurate information and references in their work.

Acknowledgment sections not only express appreciation for direct contributions but also allow authors to acknowledge the community or organizations that have supported them. For instance, authors may recognize the institutions that funded their research or the organizations that provided access to data or research facilities. This recognition helps build relationships and foster a spirit of collaboration within the academic or professional community.

In conclusion, an acknowledgment section in a book serves as a platform to express gratitude and appreciation to the various individuals who have played instrumental roles in its creation and success. From loved ones to professionals, mentors to collaborators, each person contributes to the author's growth, the refinement of ideas, and the development of the final product. Through acknowledgment, authors can publicly recognize and express heartfelt gratitude towards those who have made their writing journey a fulfilling and enriching experience.